Herbert Puchta and Jeff Stranks

English in Mind

* Student's Book 2

CAMBRIDGE
UNIVERSITY PRESS

Speaking & Functions	Listening	Reading	Writing
Describing temporary & permanent activities, past & present situations. Interview about free time.	Story about the Oregon Trail.	At the bottom of the sea. The Oregon Trail. Story: Here's my phone number.	Filling in forms.
Describing past activities. Discussion: jeans.	Stories about famous inventions. Part of a ghost story.	Young girl gets prize. Culture: Jeans.	Story about an invention.
Making comparisons. Describing a sports event. Comparing yourself with others.	Information about record-breaking sports people.	Tara's last minute win. Story: Was she pretty?	Magazine report of a sports event.
Discussing environmental problems. Predicting future events. Discussion: renewable forms of energy.	Radio interview about different forms of energy.	Our fragile planet. Culture: Energy around the world.	Website article about your town/environment.
Checking information. Talking about recently completed activities.	Quiz about Canada & the USA.	Quiz about Canada and the USA. $1000 for young Vancouver poet. Poem: Whale song. Story: You said 6.30, didn't you?	Email about a holiday.
Describing a ceremony. Retelling a story. Talking about permission. Discussion: minimum age limits.	Story about a coming of age ceremony. Dialogue about minimum ages.	From teenager to adult. Culture: Call yourself an adult?	Magazine article about a special day or ceremony.
Talking about unfinished situations. Questionnaire: Are you fun to be with? Talking about having fun.	Song: Don't Worry, Be Happy.	An interview with a clown doctor. Questionnaire: Are you fun to be with? Story: Who's going to sing?	Email about how you have fun.
Expressing likes/dislikes & preferences. Talking about films. Discussion: film stars & fame.	Dialogue about a film. Dialogue about a Hollywood star.	It was really terrifying … . Short film reviews. Culture: Hollywood lives.	Film review.
Exchanging information. A quiz. Describing a dream.	Interview about a famous earthquake.	Tsunami – the giant wave. Story: Let's talk about it later.	Newspaper story about a forest fire.
Describing quantity. Talking about your home. Discussion: stereotypes.	Descriptions of homes.	Want an adventure? Spend ten days in Borneo! An email about a holiday. Culture: Life 'down under'.	Email about a plan for a holiday.
What's your strongest intelligence? Discussing memory.	Interview about 'multiple intelligences'.	How to improve your memory. Story: The winners are … .	Competition entry.
Describing recently completed & unfinished actions. Talking about music & instruments. Discussion: pop music & fashion.	People talking about music & musical instruments.	A young winner. Culture: Pop music in Britain & the USA – a brief history.	Letter about your favourite type of music.
Expressing past habits. Exchanging information.	Dialogue at the doctor's. Dialogue about Joseph Lister.	Medicine in the past – treating headaches. Story: I used to like Joanne.	Magazine article about a famous scientist.
Giving advice. Talking about unreal situations. Discussion: computers & the Internet.	Descriptions of problems caused by computers.	Computers – good for learning, or just for fun? The Goosehead Guide to Life. Culture: Just how great are computers?	Competition entry.
Describing events in the past & earlier past. Telling a picture story.	Radio programme about the army of Xi'an.	The discovery of Machu Picchu. Story: I don't think so.	Short story.
Reporting statements & questions. Discussion: superstitions.	Dialogue about an unlucky day. Dialogue about superstitions in Britain.	A lucky break for the shoeshine boy. Culture: Where do superstitions come from?	Email to apologise for something.

Module 1
Take it to the limit

YOU WILL LEARN ABOUT ...

* Can you match each picture with a topic?

YOU WILL LEARN HOW TO ...

Speak
- Describe temporary and permanent activities
- Talk about past and present situations
- Compare yourself and others
- Talk about activities which happened in the past
- Describe similarities and differences
- Make predictions about the future
- Discuss environmental problems

Write
- Information to fill in a form
- A story about an invention
- A report about a sports event
- An article about your town environment

Read
- An article about an underwater explorer
- An article about the Oregon Trail
- Short texts about famous inventions
- An article about a young inventor
- An article about the history of jeans
- A web page about a champion snowboarder
- A text about climate changes

Listen
- A dialogue about the Oregon Trail
- Short extracts about famous inventions
- Part of a story about a mystery
- A radio interview about the environment
- Information about record breakers

Use grammar

Can you match the names of the grammar points with the examples?

Present simple vs. past simple — She **won't know unless you tell** her.

Past continuous vs. past simple — I **usually walk** to work, but yesterday I **drove**.

Comparative and superlative adjectives — I can write **more quickly than** my sister.

as ... as comparisons — These books aren't **as expensive as** those ones.

Adverbs / Comparative adverbs — James **won't go**, but Mary **might be** there.

Modal verbs for future prediction — It's a **bigger** house than mine.

First conditional and *unless* — While we **were working**, we **heard** a loud noise.

Use vocabulary

Can you think of two more examples for each topic?

Phrases with *get*	Adjectives and their opposites	The environment
get to school	easy ⟷ difficult	pollution
get angry	quiet ⟷ noisy	litter
....	....	....
....	....	....

1 Explorers

* Present simple/continuous and past simple review
* Vocabulary: guessing meaning

1 Read and listen

a Dr Robert Ballard looks for things at the bottom of the sea. What do you think he looks for? What kinds of things do you think he finds? Read the text quickly to check your ideas.

AT THE BOTTOM OF THE SEA

At the bottom of the seas and oceans, there are hundreds of shipwrecks. There are also ancient cities and settlements and one man wants to find them. His name is Dr Robert Ballard, an American who is famous for finding the Titanic about 3,800 metres down in the cold, dark waters of the North Atlantic.

Dr Ballard uses a small submarine, which he can control easily from the ship above, to explore the bottom of the sea. It has a camera that sends back live pictures of the underwater world, so that Dr Ballard can see the bottom of the sea. He sees different types of fish and coral but sometimes he finds the things he's really looking for, the remains of ancient settlements.

In 2000, Dr Ballard went to the Black Sea. But he didn't want to find a ship. 'We explored an area in the Black Sea,' he says. 'Thousands of years ago, there was land where there is water today. We found what we think is a site of human habitation down there. It may be 7,000 or 8,000 years old, and it was 100 metres under the sea.' Dr Ballard and his team are looking for more things in the site, to find out about the people who lived there.

Dr Ballard is now working on another idea – the world's first underwater museum. 'There is more history down there in the sea than in all the museums of the world,' says Ballard. 'Imagine a ship at the bottom of the sea. We can put cameras everywhere on that ship, and people all over the world can see the pictures on the Internet.'

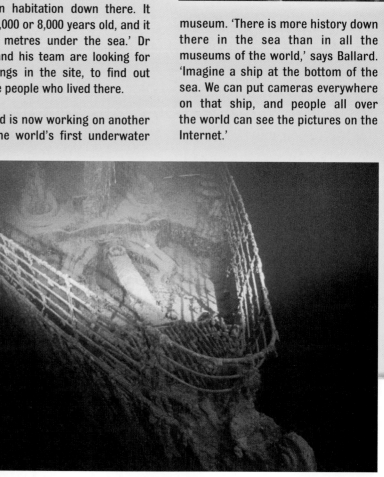

b 🔊 Read the text again and listen.

2 Vocabulary
Guessing meaning from context

a To help you understand a word, you need to know what part of speech it is. Write *noun*, *verb*, *adjective*, *adverb* or *preposition*, for each of these underlined words.

1 Dr Ballard uses a <u>small</u> submarine. *adjective*
2 There are <u>cities</u> and settlements. ....
3 One man <u>wants</u> to find them. ....
4 Imagine a ship <u>at</u> the bottom of the sea. ....
5 He can control it <u>easily</u> from above. ....

b Now find these words in the text and name the parts of speech. Can you say what each word means?

1 settlements (paragraphs 1 and 2)
2 ancient (paragraphs 1 and 2)
3 explore (paragraphs 2 and 3)
4 live (paragraph 2)
5 remains (paragraph 2)

3 Grammar
Present simple and present continuous

a Look at the examples. Then complete the rule.

*Dr Ballard **uses** a small submarine to explore the bottom of the sea.*
*Dr Ballard **is** now **working** on another idea.*

> **Rule:**
> - Use the present .... for permanent situations and routines.
> - Use the present .... to talk about actions happening now, or around now.

b Complete the summary of the text about Dr Robert Ballard on page 6. Use the present simple or present continuous form of the verbs.

Dr Robert Ballard ...*looks*... (look) for things under the sea. But he [1]............... (not go) down himself – he [2]............... (use) a small submarine. It has a camera that [3]............... (send) back pictures of the bottom of the sea.

At the moment, Dr Ballard [4]............... (not look) for a ship – he [5]............... (explore) the settlements in the Black Sea. He [6]............... also .... (work) on an idea for an underwater museum.

c Here are some answers to questions about the text on page 6. Write the questions.

1 *Where is Dr Ballard from*............... ?
   He's from America.
2 .... ?
   He is a scientist and explorer. He explores the bottom of the sea.
3 .... there?
   He finds shipwrecks and ancient settlements.
4 .... ?
   He uses a small submarine.
5 .... ?
   It sends live pictures of the bottom of the sea to Dr Ballard.
6 .... shipwrecks?
   No, he isn't. He's looking for settlements.
7 .... ?
   He's working on an idea for a museum.

4 Speak

Work with a partner. Student A: read the information about Kevin Hayes on this page. Student B: turn to page 122. Ask and answer questions to complete your missing information. Student A: you start.

Student A: *Where does Kevin live?*

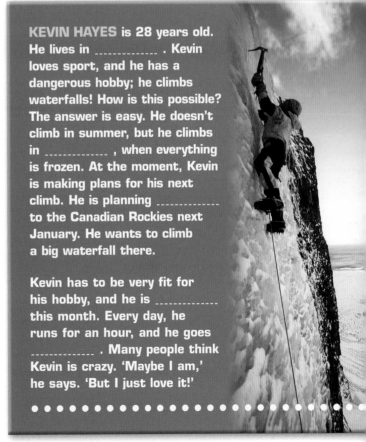

KEVIN HAYES is 28 years old. He lives in .... Kevin loves sport, and he has a dangerous hobby; he climbs waterfalls! How is this possible? The answer is easy. He doesn't climb in summer, but he climbs in .... , when everything is frozen. At the moment, Kevin is making plans for his next climb. He is planning .... to the Canadian Rockies next January. He wants to climb a big waterfall there.

Kevin has to be very fit for his hobby, and he is .... this month. Every day, he runs for an hour, and he goes .... Many people think Kevin is crazy. 'Maybe I am,' he says. 'But I just love it!'

5 Read and listen

a Look at the pictures and answer the questions.

1. Which states did the Oregon Trail go through?
2. How long was the trail, do you think?
3. How long do you think a journey took along the Oregon Trail?
4. What problems do you think people had on the journey?

b Read the text and check your answers.

c 🔊 Listen to Karen and Mark talking about an accident that happened on the Oregon Trail. What happened? How did it happen?

d 🔊 Complete the summary. Then listen again and check your answers.

The accident happened in the year [1] .... The settlers were in the boat because they wanted to [2] ...., but the boat was too full and it turned over and sank. [3] .... people died. Too many people were on the boat because the people who had the boats wanted to make [4] .... The settlers paid [5] .... each to get in the boat.

THE OREGON TRAIL

In the 19th century, millions of Europeans emigrated to the USA because they wanted to find a better life. Many of them couldn't find work in cities like New York, so they left and went to find farmland in the west. The people, called settlers, travelled west through the mountains on the 'Oregon Trail'.

Map: Washington, Oregon, Idaho, Wyoming, Nebraska, Kansas, Missouri, California, Oregon Trail. N

Some of these people hoped to find gold in California. The journey sometimes took more than a year. There are a lot of films, called 'Westerns', about the settlers on the trail. In most of the films, we see the Native Americans ('American Indians') attacking the settlers, and the 'Indians' kill thousands of white people. But the truth is that the Native Americans were not the biggest problem for the settlers. In fact, most of them were very helpful to the settlers.

It is true that the settlers' journey was extremely difficult. Many of them walked 3,200 kilometres, the whole length of the trail. They had wagons, but the wagons were often too full, so people could not travel in them. Many parents also had to carry their small children. The people were very poor and many did not even have shoes – they walked the whole trail barefoot, in extremely cold temperatures.

More than 50,000 people, including many women and children, died on the trail. A lot of people died from illnesses like cholera, because the drinking water wasn't clean. There were also a lot of accidents. Many people died under the wheels of wagons, for example, and from accidental gunshots.

6 Grammar

Past simple: regular and irregular verbs

a) Underline examples of past simple regular verbs in the text on page 8. Then complete the rule.

> **Rule:**
> - To form the past simple of most regular verbs, add
>   _____ . If a regular verb ends in a consonant plus *y*
>   (*study, carry* etc.), add _____ .
> - To form questions in the past simple, use *did* + the
>   _____ without *to*.

b) Complete the table. Check with the list of irregular verbs on page 124.

be	*was/were*	find	_____	see	_____
can	_____	go	_____	sink	_____
catch	_____	have	_____	take	_____
come	_____	leave	_____	write	_____

c) Here are some answers to questions about the text on page 8. Complete the questions.

1 Why *did millions of people go to America in the 19th century* ?
   Because they wanted to find a better way of life there.

2 Where _____ ?
   They went west, through the mountains along the Oregon Trail.

3 Why _____ ?
   Because they couldn't find work in the cities.

4 How long _____ ?
   It took more than a year.

5 _____ ?
   Because the wagons were too full.

6 _____ ?
   More than 50,000 people.

d) Complete the summary of the text on page 8. Use the past simple form of the verbs.

Before 1900, many people ____*left*____ (leave) Europe because they [1]_____ (hope) to find a new life in America. Some people [2]_____ (make) new homes in cities, but others [3]_____ (not find) work, so they [4]_____ (decide) to walk west along the Oregon Trail to find work on farmland. The journey [5]_____ (be) very hard and sometimes they [6]_____ (travel) for a year.

The settlers [7]_____ (use) wagons to carry their things, but the wagons [8]_____ (not have) a lot of space, so many people [9]_____ (walk) and they [10]_____ (carry) their small children. Some people [11]_____ (not have) shoes, so they [12]_____ (go) barefoot. Many people [13]_____ (die) along the way. A lot of people [14]_____ (catch) diseases like cholera and others [15]_____ (have) accidents.

7 Pronunciation

Linking sounds in the past simple

🔊 Turn to page 120.

8 Speak

Work with a partner. Ask and answer questions. Use the present and past simple, and the topics in the box below.

A: *Where do you usually go on holiday?*
B: *I usually go to the beach.*
A: *Did you like your holiday last year?*
B: *Yes, it was great!*

> Sport   Music   TV
> Weekends   Holidays

> Where ... ?
> What ... play?
> When ... start?
> What ... last ... ?
> Who ... with?
> How often ... ?
> Do/Did... ?

Here's my phone number

9 Read and listen

a 🔊 Where are the people in the story? Who works there? Who is a customer? Read, listen and check your answers.

Dave: Hi. Can I help you?

Joanne: No, I'm just looking, thanks.

Dave: OK. If you need any help, my name's Dave.

Joanne: Hi, Dave. I'm Joanne.

Dave: I see you're looking at Ani DiFranco CDs. Do you like her music?

Joanne: Too right! Her last album was brilliant.

Dave: Yeah, I thought it was cool, too.

Joanne: So, we like the same kind of music.

Dave: Yeah. Do you live round here?

Joanne: Yes, just a few streets away. And do you work here every day?

Dave: No, only on Saturdays. I'm still at school. Highgrove Comprehensive.

Joanne: Isn't that Nick's school? The bloke from 4Tune?

Dave: That's right. Actually, I'm trying to get a band together myself. I play guitar, my girlfriend Amy sings ... We're going to enter a competition for new bands, in four weeks' time, in London.

Joanne: Really?

Dave: Yeah. The band that wins gets the chance to make a CD with a record company. Then if the record company like it they may give the band a recording contract!

Joanne: Brilliant! Look, if you need a keyboard player, call me. I'm not bad. I sing a bit too.

Dave: All right, I will. Did you say your name's Joanne?

Joanne: Yes, Joanne Willis. Look, here's my phone number ...

Mr Dobson: Dave! Come on! I'm not paying you to do nothing, you know!

Dave: OK, Mr Dobson. I'm coming!

b Mark the statements *T* (true) or *F* (false).

1 Both Dave and Joanne like Ani DiFranco's music. ☐

2 Joanne lives far away from the shop. ☐

3 Dave works in the record shop twice a week. ☐

4 Dave goes to the same school as Nick. ☐

5 In four months' time there will be a competition for new bands. ☐

6 The first prize in the competition is a recording contract. ☐

7 Joanne wants to join Dave's band. ☐

10 Everyday English

(a) Find expressions 1–4 in the story. Who says them?

1   Too right!
2   Do you live round here?
3   The bloke from 4Tune?
4   Actually, I'm trying to get a band together …

(b) How do you say *actually* in your language?

(c) Match the underlined expressions 1–3 from the story with definitions a–c.

1   Too right!   a   (young) man
2   round here   b   in this area
3   bloke   c   yes, that's true

(d) Complete the sentences with the underlined words from Exercise 10a.

1   Luisa: There's a new club in town.
    Marco: That's great, because there isn't much to do ....

2   Clare: Don't you think Tom's a bit strange?
    Jane: Well no, I think he's a really nice ....
    I like him a lot.

3   Marta: I love Bon Jovi.
    Sue: Really? I don't like their music very much.
    .... I think it's terrible!

4   Maria: This programme's really boring!
    Ben: .... ! Let's watch something else.

11 Write

Filling in forms

(a) Match the questions 1–5 with the words a–e from a form.

1   What is your family name?   a   Sex (male or female)
2   When were you born?   b   Address
3   Where are you from?   c   Date of birth
4   Are you a boy or a girl?   d   Surname
5   Where do you live?   e   Nationality

(b) Imagine that you want to do an English course at an English language college in Britain. Fill in the enrolment form.

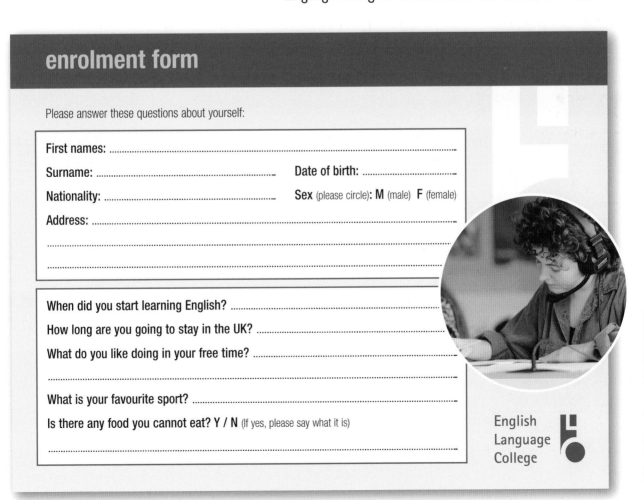

enrolment form

Please answer these questions about yourself:

First names: ....

Surname: ....   Date of birth: ....

Nationality: ....   Sex (please circle): **M** (male) **F** (female)

Address: ....
....
....

When did you start learning English? ....

How long are you going to stay in the UK? ....

What do you like doing in your free time? ....
....

What is your favourite sport? ....

Is there any food you cannot eat? **Y / N** (If yes, please say what it is)
....

English
Language
College

2 That's an idea!

* Past continuous
* Past continuous vs. past simple, *when/while*
* Vocabulary: phrases with *get*

1 Read and listen

(a) Match the words in the box with the pictures. Write 1–8 in the boxes.

1 crisps
2 traffic lights
3 wig
4 cat's eyes
5 typewriter
6 biro™
7 hair dye
8 TV

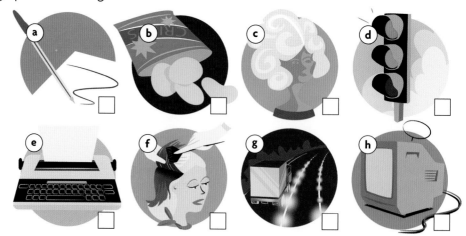

(b) Read the texts. What do you think each person invented? Choose from the objects in Exercise 1a.

(c) 🔊 Listen to the complete stories and check your answers.

It was 1933 and Percy Shaw, from England, was driving home at night along a dark road. He was worried because it was raining and he couldn't see very well. Then he saw something in the middle of the road.

In 1853, in a restaurant in New York, people were having dinner. A man was eating fried potatoes, but he didn't like them. He called for the cook and told him that the potatoes were too thick. The cook, George Crum, got angry.

In the 1920s in Scotland, John Logie Baird and a friend were talking on the phone. Baird thought the telephone was an amazing invention. While he was listening to his friend, he began to think, 'I'd really like to invent a machine like this – but for the eye, not for the ear.'

In 1907, a French chemist called Eugene Schueller was talking to a woman in his shop. She was getting older and her hair was going grey.

In 1935, in a newspaper office in Budapest, a young Hungarian reporter was writing a story for the next day. He was unhappy with his pen because while he was writing, he had to stop many times to fill it with ink. And so he started to think.

(d) 🔊 Listen again and answer the questions.

1 What did Percy Shaw see in the middle of the road?
2 Why was George Crum surprised?
3 Why was the French woman unhappy?
4 What was the young Hungarian's family name?

2 Grammar

Past continuous

a Look at the examples.

*Percy Shaw **was driving** home at night ...*
*... people **were having** dinner ...*

b <u>Underline</u> other examples of the past continuous in the texts on page 12. Then read the rule and complete the table.

Positive	Negative	Question	Short answer
I/he/she/it .... working	I/he/she/it .... (was not) working	.... I/he/she/it working?	Yes, I/he/she/it .... No, I/he/she/it .... (was not).
you/we/they .... working	you/we/they **weren't** (were not) working	.... you/we/they working?	Yes, you/we/they .... No, you/we/they .... (were not).

Rule: Use the past continuous to talk about actions in progress at a certain time in the past.

c Yesterday Helen went to a party. What were her friends doing when she arrived? Fill in the spaces with the verbs in the box.

> dance   ~~listen~~   sit   drink   talk

1 Marco *was listening* to the music.

2 Hugo and Anna .... together.

3 Kemal .... on the sofa.

4 Marco and Kemal .... fruit juice.

5 Luisa .... on her mobile .

d Complete the sentences. Use the past continuous form of the verbs.

1 A: Where ...*were you going*... (you/go) when I saw you this morning?

   B: I .... (run) to my friend's house. I was late and she .... (wait) for me.

2 A: What .... (you/do) when I phoned you?

   B: I .... (watch) TV.

3 A: .... (your parents / live) in Italy when you were born?

   B: No, they .... (live) in London. My father .... (work) for the Italian Embassy.

4 A: .... (your sister / dance) with Maria at the party last night?

   B: Yes, she was. They .... (dance) all night.

5 A: Who .... (you/play) tennis with yesterday?

   B: I .... (play) with Paolo. He's very good!

3 Pronunciation

was and *were*

🔊 Turn to page 120.

4 Speak

a Work with a partner. Ask and answer questions about the picture.

A: *Was Kemal **sleeping** on the sofa?*

B: *No, he **wasn't**. He **was drinking** fruit juice.*

b Ask your partner what he/she was doing at different times yesterday.

A: *What **were** you **doing** at seven o'clock yesterday morning?*

B: *I **was having** breakfast.*

5 Listen

a Read the beginning of a short story. What do you think happened after the boy went out of the cave?

THE BOY IN THE CAVE

One day, I was going for a walk in a forest. I was walking through the trees, when suddenly I found a cave. It looked very dark inside. I wasn't sure if I should go in or not. While I was thinking, I heard a noise in the cave. There was somebody inside! I went into the cave and I saw a small boy. He was sitting on the floor and he was crying. I took his hand and we went outside …

b 🔊 Listen to the rest of the story. Check your ideas from Exercise 5a.

c What do you think happened to the boy and the dog?

6 Grammar

Past continuous vs. past simple

a Look at the sentence from the story. Underline the past continuous verbs and circle the past simple verb.

I was walking through the trees, when suddenly I found a cave.

b Look at the diagram. Which sentence tells us the background action? Which sentence tells us what happened at one moment? Complete the rule.

I was walking through the trees,

→

I found a cave.

....
Rule:
* Use the .... for a background action or description.
* Use the .... for an action that happened at one particular moment.
....

c Look at the sentences from the story. Complete them with the correct form of the verbs.

1 While we .... (walk), he .... (start) to cry again.
2 We .... (get) close to the town, when suddenly the boy .... (stop).
3 The boy .... (not be) there, but a small white dog .... (sit) on the ground.

when and *while*

d Look at the sentences from the story. Then complete the rule.

*I was walking through the trees **when** suddenly I **found** a cave.*
***While** I **was thinking**, I heard a noise inside the cave.*

....
Rule: We often use *when* with the past .... and *while* with the past ....
....

e Complete the sentences. Use the past simple or past continuous form of the verbs.

1 I *was writing* (write) an email. The phone *rang* (ring).
2 Harry .... (run) to school. He .... (fall) and hurt his leg.
3 Alex and Sue .... (play) tennis. Lucy .... (arrive).
4 Antonio .... (have) breakfast. He .... (have) a great idea.
5 Carlo .... (talk) on the phone. His father .... (go) out.

f Join the sentences in Exercise 6e in two different ways. Use *when* and *while*.

*I was writing an email **when** the phone rang.*
***While** I was writing an email, the phone rang.*

7 Read

a Look at the pictures. Sarah Hutchins won a prize for inventing something. What do you think it was? Read the first two paragraphs of the text quickly to check your answer.

Young girl gets prize

Sarah Hutchins has won a great prize from Amazon.com in a competition for young inventors.

Sarah invented 'camoculars' – binoculars and a camera together. She was one of thousands of young people who sent their ideas to Amazon.com, the web company that organised the competition for young inventors.

Sarah was at a concert when she thought of her invention. 'I was sitting a long way from the stage and I was watching the band through my binoculars. While I was watching, I thought, "I'd love to be able to take a picture of this!" Then I got an idea. Why not have binoculars with a camera inside them?'

When she got home, she took some plastic binoculars and a cheap camera and put them

together. Her sister was watching her and told her about the competition. So Sarah sent her idea to Amazon.com and two months later, she got a surprise. Amazon.com phoned to say that she was a winner. They didn't give her the top prize in the competition, but she won $1,000 and a trip to New York.

People are already asking Sarah what she is going to invent next. 'I don't know,' says Sarah. 'If you just sit there and think, you won't invent anything, because you get ideas at strange moments. The only thing I can do is keep my eyes and ears open!'

b Read the whole text and match the two parts of the sentences.

1 Sarah Hutchins got a prize   a   was watching a concert.
2 She got the idea when she   b   idea to the web company.
3 At home she put   c   invited her to New York.
4 Then she sent her   d   what she is going to invent next.
5 They liked her idea a lot and   e   for inventing 'camoculars'.
6 Sarah is thinking about   f   binoculars and a camera together.

c What do you think of Sarah's invention? Do you think it's a good idea?

8 Vocabulary

get

a The verb *get* can mean *arrive*, *receive* or *become*. Look at the phrases from texts in this unit. Write the meaning of *get* in each sentence.

1 The cook **got** angry.
= *became*

2 We were **getting** close to the town. = _____

3 She was **getting** older.
= _____

4 Sarah **got** home.
= _____

5 She **got** a surprise.
= _____

6 You **get** ideas at strange moments.
= _____

b Complete the sentences with the words in the box. Use the past simple or past continuous forms.

get wet   get a surprise
get to school
~~get the answer~~
get an idea   get angry

1 The Maths question was very hard, but in the end I *got the answer*.

2 I woke up at 8.30 this morning, so I _____ really late.

3 Alex stopped playing football because it was raining and he _____ .

4 I was trying to decide what to buy for my sister's birthday. But then I _____ .

5 My teacher _____ because I didn't do my homework.

6 Last week my father _____ . He won $1,000 in the lottery!

Culture in mind

9 Read

a) Look at the pictures. Who do you think the man is? When do you think jeans became fashionable? Read the magazine article to check your answers.

Jeans are popular all over the world – millions of people wear them every day. But who invented them, and when did they become fashionable?

Levi Strauss – a name that is now famous – was the man who invented jeans. Levi Strauss was born in Germany in 1829, but went to the USA as a young man. At first he lived in New York, but in 1853 he moved to San Francisco, where he worked with his

brother. They worked in a shop selling clothes to men who were looking for gold in the California Gold Rush. The men were working very hard in difficult conditions, and they needed very strong trousers.

Strauss was the first man to begin producing special, strong trousers for working men. He made these trousers from a fabric called 'denim' – a tough fabric that probably came from a town called Nîmes in France. Many people now think the English word 'denim' comes from the French words 'de Nîmes', which means 'from Nîmes'. Later, Strauss added special metal buttons to the trousers to make them even better and they immediately became very popular.

In the early part of the 20th century, only working men wore jeans in workplaces like factories. But after the Second World War, teenage boys and young men at college started to wear them to go out. These boys called the trousers 'jeans'. In the 1960s, more young Americans started wearing them as informal, casual clothes outside the workplace and denim jeans became fashionable. In the 1960s and 1970s, 'decorated denim' became very popular. These are jeans decorated with sequins, beads, colours and patterns.

At that time, jeans were usually flared, but today, there are many different styles of jeans; straight, baggy, flared, low-waisted – almost any style you can imagine.

Today, millions of people wear jeans to go to work in offices, as well as to go out. Jeans are as popular today as they ever were, but there is one thing no one is really sure about – why are they called 'jeans'?

b) Choose the best title for the article.

1. From workwear to fashion
2. Why are jeans so popular?
3. Jeans around the world

c) Answer the questions.

1. When and where was Levi Strauss born?
2. Why did he move from New York to California?
3. Who wore the first denim jeans?
4. Where do some people think the word 'denim' comes from?
5. What is it that no one knows about jeans?

Discussion box

Work in pairs or small groups.
Discuss these questions together.

1 How popular are jeans in your country?
2 How many pairs of jeans have you got?
3 Where do people usually wear jeans in your country? (work? school? restaurants? clubs?)
4 What style(s) of jeans are most popular with your age group? (straight? baggy? flared?)
5 Do you like jeans? Why / Why not?

10 Write

a Read Alex's story about an invention and answer questions 1–3.

1 What's the name of the invention and who invented it? ☐
2 Why is it a good invention? ☐
3 When and how did the inventor get the idea? ☐

b Match the questions in Exercise 10a with the paragraphs. Write A, B and C in the boxes.

A I'm going to write about the tape called Velcro™. The man who invented it was George de Mestral, from Switzerland.

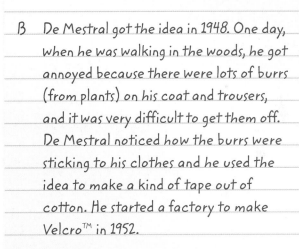

B De Mestral got the idea in 1948. One day, when he was walking in the woods, he got annoyed because there were lots of burrs (from plants) on his coat and trousers, and it was very difficult to get them off. De Mestral noticed how the burrs were sticking to his clothes and he used the idea to make a kind of tape out of cotton. He started a factory to make Velcro™ in 1952.

C I think Velcro™ is very useful for things like trainers and other clothes and also for bags, because it's easy and quick to use.

c Write a story about an invention. Use Alex's story to help you.

③ She jumped well

✳ Comparative and superlative adjectives
✳ Intensifiers with comparatives
✳ (not) as ... as
✳ Adverbs / comparative adverbs
✳ Vocabulary: antonyms

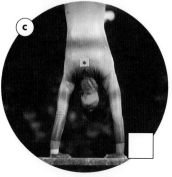

1 Listen

(a) Match the names of the sports with the pictures. Write 1–4 in the boxes.

> 1 high jump 2 free diving
> 3 long jump 4 gymnastics

(b) 🔊 Look at the profiles. What sport do you think each athlete does? Write the names of the sports in the spaces. Then listen and complete the information about the athletes.

BREAKING RECORDS

NADIA COMANECI

⭐ born: 1961
⭐ sport: _____
⭐ perfect score: _____ points.
⭐ Olympics 1976: got _____ perfect scores and won _____ gold medals.
⭐ She was _____ years old, _____ than most of the other athletes, but she wasn't the _____ athlete. Robin Consiglia won silver when she was only _____ .

RAYMOND EWRY

⭐ 1874–1937
⭐ sports: _____ and _____
⭐ 1900–1908: _____ gold medals.
⭐ Ewry was the _____ successful athlete in Olympic history.
⭐ No other athlete has as _____ gold medals as Ewry.
⭐ Today's athletes _____ much _____ and _____ than Ewry.
⭐ Records: 1.65 metres in the _____ and _____ metres in the _____ .

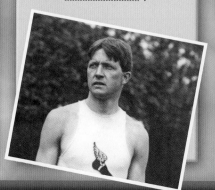

PIPIN & AUDREY FERRERAS

⭐ Pipin born: 1964
  Audrey: 1974–2002
⭐ sport: _____
⭐ Pipin's record: _____ metres.
⭐ Pipin believes he can go _____, perhaps as _____ as 200 metres.
⭐ Audrey's record: _____ metres.

2 Grammar

Comparative and superlative adjectives

a Look at the example. <u>Underline</u> more examples of comparative and superlative adjectives in the text on page 18.

*She wasn't **the youngest** athlete.*

b Put the adjectives in the box below in the correct columns. How do you form the comparative and superlative of *far* and *bad*?

-er/-est	-ier/-iest	more/most	Irregular comparatives
young	easy	successful	far

> fat   ~~easy~~   bad   tidy   ~~young~~   ~~far~~   fast   quiet
> interesting   ~~successful~~   high   deep   new

Intensifiers with comparative adjectives

*Sue's **much / far / a lot** younger than Anna.*

*The green bike is **a bit / a little** cheaper than the red one.*

c Compare the things in the sentences. Use *much / far / a lot*, or *a bit / a little*.

1 watching TV / reading a book (interesting / easy)
   I think watching TV is far more interesting than reading a book.
2 a computer / a mobile phone (expensive / useful)
3 boys / girls (intelligent / tidy)
4 English / History (difficult / easy)
5 my father / my mother (young / tall)
6 The Atlantic ocean / the Pacific ocean (deep / big)

3 Vocabulary and grammar

Antonyms

a Match adjectives 1–12 with their opposites in Exercise 2b. How do you form the comparative and superlative of adjectives 1–12?

1 unsuccessful *successful*
2 slim ....
3 boring ....
4 shallow ....
5 low ....
6 slow ....
7 noisy ....
8 messy ....
9 difficult ....
10 near ....
11 good ....
12 old .... / ....

as ... as comparatives

b We can use (*not*) *as ... as* to compare things. Look at the examples. Then <u>underline</u> other examples of *as ... as* in the text on page 18.

*My sister **isn't as tall as** me.*
*= My sister's **shorter** than me.*

*Tom's feet **are as big as** his father's feet.*
*= Tom's feet are **the same size as** his father's feet.*

c Complete the second sentence so it means the same as the first.

1 Sarah's brother is younger than Sarah.
   Sarah's brother isn't *as old as* Sarah.
2 Peter's messier than his sister.
   Peter isn't .... his sister.
3 Travelling by train is often faster than travelling by bus.
   Travelling by train isn't .... travelling by bus.
4 My dog is much noisier than my cat.
   My dog isn't .... my cat.
5 Jo thinks English is easier than French.
   Jo thinks English isn't .... French.
6 For me, reading is more interesting than watching TV.
   For me, watching TV .... reading.

4 Pronunciation

than and *as*

🔊 Turn to page 120.

5 Read

a Look at the pictures and the title. What's the name of the sport? Did Tara win the competition? Read the text quickly to check your ideas.

b Mark the statements *T* (true) or *F* (false).

1 Before her last jump, Tara was in second place. ☐

2 Tara's last jump was a 540° turn. ☐

3 Tara's last jump was better because she wasn't as nervous as before. ☐

4 In her last jump, Tara went faster than in the other two jumps. ☐

5 Tara is now going to practise hard all weekend. ☐

Tara's Last-Minute Win

More than 7,000 people saw a dramatic third and last round of the women's Big Air contest at the Winter X Games at Mount Snow, Vermont. Tara Dakides, a regular winner of top events, won with the very last jump of the competition.

After the first two jumps, Barrett Christy was in first place, with Tara in tenth position. In the last round, Tara watched nervously as Christy did her final jump. Christy jumped well, and Tara knew that her third and last jump had to be good. She jumped brilliantly, a 540° turn, and the scores came up quickly on the board. They told everyone that Tara was the winner and had her first Gold Medal of the week.

'In the first two rounds I jumped badly', said Tara. 'But in the third round, when I heard the people shouting "Tara! Tara!" I relaxed, you know, and I jumped well, much better than before.'

She said the most important thing in the last jump was that she was more confident. 'I practise this jump regularly and I know I can do it. So I went down the hill fast, you know, a lot more quickly than the first two times, and it worked! I don't like waiting until the last jump to win, but it's OK, I won, and I'm happy. It wasn't easy, but in these competitions you never win easily.'

Tara's going to party a little over the weekend, and then she's going to the next big snowboarding event at Mammoth Mountain, California. Maybe she'll win again, and more easily next time, but Christy will be there too. Who will be the winner next time?

6 Grammar

Adverbs, comparative adverbs

a Look at the examples. Underline other examples of adverbs in the text on page 20.

*Tara watched **nervously**.*
*Christy jumped **well**.*

b How do you form the adverbs of:
- regular adjectives (for example, *quick*)?
- adjectives ending in y (for example, *easy*)?
- *fast* and *good*?

c Read Mark's diary. Then (circle) the correct words.

May 4th

Last night, my father was talking about languages. He's crazy. He says that he speaks French good / (well,) but he doesn't. I've heard him speaking French: he tries to speak very ¹ quick / quickly, and his pronunciation is ² terrible / terribly. But I didn't tell him that.

I want to speak a language ³ fluent / fluently. Yesterday I talked to our teacher, Miss Girard, about my French test. She said my score was 4 out of 20 – I did the test really ⁴ bad / badly. I don't understand it. I thought the test was ⁵ easy / easily and I answered all the questions really ⁶ quick / quickly.

Miss Girard said I'll never be ⁷ good / well at French, but I smiled ⁸ happy / happily at her, because she's beautiful. I'm going to learn French and then I'm going to marry her.

d Look at these examples of comparative adverbs from the text on page 20. Then complete the rule.

*I went down the hill **more quickly than** the first two times.*
*Maybe she'll win again, and **more easily** next time.*

> **Rule:** To form the comparative of most adverbs, add the word .... before the adverb.

e Some comparative adverbs add *-er/-ier* to the adverb, others change completely. Complete the examples.

soon	*sooner*	hard	....		
fast	....	early	*earlier*		
good	....	bad	....	far	*further*

f Complete the sentences. Write the comparative adverbs of the adjectives.

1 Sue ran *more quickly* (quick) than Alison.
2 Pedro speaks English .... (fluent) than me.
3 Alex writes .... (clear) than Martha.
4 My sister swims .... (fast) than me.
5 Ken always works .... (hard) than everyone else.
6 Tom usually passes his exams .... (easy) than his friends.
7 Jem and Sam both did well in the test, but Jem did even .... (good) than Sam.
8 My friend has to travel .... (far) than me to get to school.

7 Speak

Work with a partner. Compare yourself to your family and friends. Use the verbs in the box.

A: *I can swim faster than my brother.*
B: *My older sister speaks English better than me.*

| run | swim | write | sing | speak |
| type | .... (your idea) | | | |

Was she pretty?

8 Read and listen

(a) 🔊 Who are the two people in the story? Where are they?
What are they talking about? Read, listen and check your answers.

Amy: How was work today, Dave?

Dave: Well, not as good as last week. Dobson had a go at me.

Amy: No way! Why?

Dave: Just because I was talking to a customer in the shop. A girl called Joanne.

Amy: Oh really? Was she pretty?

Dave: Oh, Amy – stop it, please!

Amy: So, what were you talking to her about?

Dave: Well, we got talking about music. Then I told her about our idea for a band, and she said she plays keyboards.

Amy: Well we need a keyboard player. What's her name again?

Dave: Joanne Willis. She's a bit older than us, I think. And, er ... she sings, too.

Amy: Hold on, Dave. I'm the singer, remember?

Dave: Of course you are, Amy. You're the best singer in town!

Amy: Oh Dave! And don't forget – we still need a drummer.

Dave: Actually, no. I found one. A bloke called Matt. He answered the advert I put in the newspaper. He's coming to the rehearsal tomorrow.

Amy: Great!

Dave: And, er, Amy – I phoned Joanne half an hour ago, and I invited her too. OK?

Amy: Oh, I see ... But why didn't you ask me first?

Dave: Oh Amy, I'm sorry, don't get angry.

Amy: Listen, Dave, I'm off now. I'll see you tomorrow at the rehearsal.

Dave: But Amy, aren't we going to talk ...? Oh ... bye then.

(b) Answer the questions.

1 Why was Dave's day at work not as good as last week?
2 Why do you think Dave asks Amy to 'stop it'?
3 Amy isn't very happy when Dave says that Joanne sings. Why not?
4 How did Dave find a drummer for the band?
5 Why do you think Amy goes home?

9 Everyday English

a Find expressions 1–4 in the story. Who says them? Match them with definitions a–d.

1 had a go at me   a I'm leaving
2 Stop it!   b got angry with me
3 Hold on.   c be quiet!
4 I'm off.   d wait

b Complete the sentences with the underlined words from Exercise 9a.

1 Susie: Goodbye, ... See you later.
   Clare: Bye, see you.
2 Mark: So, tell me. Are you going out with Clare, or not?
   Ben: Oh, ... , Mark! I told you I don't want to talk about it.
3 Julia: What's wrong, Anna?
   Anna: I was late for school again and my teacher ....
4 John: Right, let's go.
   Lukas: .... ! I can't find my shoes.

10 Speak and write

a Tom's teacher asked him to write a report about a sports event. Read Tom's report and answer the questions.

1 What kind of event was it?
2 When and where did it take place?
3 How did the players and teams play?
4 Who scored the goals for England?
5 What was the final result?
6 Did he enjoy the event? Why / Why not?

b Read Tom's report again and match the topics 1–3 with the paragraphs. Write A, B and C in the boxes.

1 What happened at the event   ☐
2 Tom's opinion of the event   ☐
3 General information about the event ☐

c Work with a partner. Think about a sports event you have watched. Tell each other about the event. Use the questions in Exercise 10a to help you.

A Last Saturday afternoon, I went to an exciting football match in London. My dad got me a ticket for the final against Holland.

B The match was really exciting from the start. Holland scored a goal after ten minutes, and they were playing really well. They almost scored two more goals in the first half, but after half time, England played better. Rooney, my favourite player, was excellent. After sixty minutes, he scored the first goal, and ten minutes later he scored another goal and the score was 2–1! I think Rooney's the best player. He plays better, runs faster and shoots harder than all the other players.

C The final score was 2–1 to England. I think it was a great match. England played brilliantly! My dad and I were very excited, and very happy because our team won. After the match, we went and had a pizza together. It was a great day.

d Write a report for your school magazine about the event you watched. Use Tom's report and the questions in Exercise 10a to help you.

For your portfolio

4 Our world

* *will/won't, might / may (not)*
* First conditional, *unless*
* Vocabulary: the environment

1 Read and listen

(a) Look at the photos and the title. How is the world's climate changing? Read the text to check your ideas.

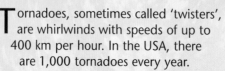

Our fragile planet

Tornadoes, sometimes called 'twisters', are whirlwinds with speeds of up to 400 km per hour. In the USA, there are 1,000 tornadoes every year. They look fascinating and dramatic when we are watching them on TV, but they can kill. In Britain, there were very few tornadoes in the past. Now, there are more than 50 tornadoes a year.

Tornadoes are only one sign of the world's climate changes. There are many others. The number of thunderstorms is increasing and there are more hurricanes. There are more floods in some parts of the world, and there's much less rain in others. We know that these things happen because global temperatures are rising and many people believe the weather will get worse in the future. The problems of climate change won't go away unless we do something about the causes.

Scientists still do not know enough about the reasons for these temperature changes. Some say that these types of climate changes are natural, but most scientists think human activity is the problem. Cutting down trees, burning too much oil, and the increase in the number of cars and planes are some of the things that cause the problems.

Scientists believe that if the temperatures continue to rise, the ice at the poles will melt. If the ice melts, sea levels will rise. Some islands might disappear completely, and there might be floods in coastal cities. All this means that unless we do something to stop global warming now, there may be many other dramatic changes in the future.

(b) 🔊 Read the text again and listen. Match the two parts of the sentences.

1 The weather is changing around the world
2 Most scientists think
3 If the ice at the poles continues to melt
4 There might be even more problems in future

a if we don't do something now.
b sea levels will go up even more.
c because temperatures are rising.
d the climate changes are not natural.

2 Vocabulary

The environment

a What is the meaning of the <u>underlined</u> words from the text on page 24?

(paragraph 2)

1 the number of thunderstorms is <u>increasing</u>

2 temperatures are <u>rising</u>

(paragraph 4)

3 the ice at the <u>poles</u> will <u>melt</u>

4 islands might <u>disappear</u>

5 <u>floods</u> in <u>coastal</u> cities

6 <u>global warming</u>

b 🔊 Match the words with the pictures. Write 1–8 in the boxes. Then listen, check and repeat.

1 recycling
2 litter
3 pollution
4 factory fumes
5 rainforests
6 the atmosphere
7 rubbish
8 a power station

c Complete the sentences with the verbs in the box.

waste   ~~drop~~   clean up
recycle   pick up
cut down   pollute

1 Don't _drop_ litter. Someone has to _____ it _____!

2 We will _____ your empty bottles. Leave them here.

3 Water is important, so don't _____ it.

4 Every year, people have to _____ thousands of tonnes of oil from beaches.

5 Factories and power stations _____ the air we breathe and our water.

6 Every year, people _____ 78 million acres of rainforest, an area larger than Poland.

a
b
c
d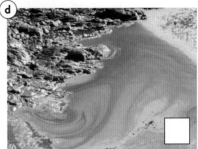
e
f
g
h

3 Speak

a Work with a partner. Make a list of problems in the environment where you live.

There are a lot of cars, and a lot of air pollution.
There is a lot of litter on the streets.

b Put your list in order of how serious you think the problems are. Number 1 is the most serious. Compare your list with other pairs.

c Now make another list of things ordinary people can do to improve the environment.

I think we should use bicycles or walk for short journeys.
We should recycle our bottles and rubbish.

d Which of the things in your list do you do now?

4 Grammar

will/won't, and *might / may (not)* for prediction

a Look at the examples. <u>Underline</u> other examples of *will/won't* and *might (not) / may (not)* in the text on page 24. Then complete the rule.

*The weather **will get** worse in the future.*
*Some islands **might disappear** completely.*

> **Rule:** Use .... or *(won't)* to express certainty and .... *(not)* or *may (not)* to express possibility.

b Complete the sentences. Use *will, 'll,* or *won't* and the verbs.

1 Great! The weather man on TV says it <u>will be</u> (be) sunny tomorrow.

2 Do you think people in the future .... (travel) to other planets like Mars?

3 What time .... we .... (arrive) in New York tomorrow, do you think?

4 I love those trainers! When I get my pocket money next week, I think I .... (buy) them.

5 Please can you help me with my homework? I promise it .... (take) very long.

c Complete the sentences. Use *might* or *might not* and the verbs.

1 Don't give that ice cream to the cat! It <u>might be</u> (be) sick!

2 A: Where's Alicia?
B: I'm not sure. I think she .... (be) in her piano lesson.

3 I don't know if this book is a good present for my brother. He .... (like) it.

4 Don't put that glass there! Someone .... (break) it.

5 I'm worried about my Maths test tomorrow. I .... (pass) it!

6 In the future, people will probably travel in space and they .... (live) on other planets.

7 I feel awful, I think I .... (have) flu.

d (Circle) the correct words.

1 I don't think you should throw your skis away. You (might) / might not need them later.

2 You don't need to take a jumper, it *will / won't* be cold there.

3 There's a lot of traffic today, we *might / might not* be late for school.

4 Take your umbrella. I'm sure it *will / may* rain soon.

5 I have no definite plans for my holiday, but I *will / might* go to Scotland for a few days.

6 A: Do you think France *will / might* win?
B: They *will /might*, but Holland are a very good team too.

7 Anne is ill, so I'm sure she *may not / won't* go to the party on Saturday.

5 Pronunciation

/əʊ/ *won't*

🔊 Turn to page 120.

6 Speak

Work with a partner. Talk about life in the future, 100 years from now. Make predictions. Use *will/won't* and *might (not) / may (not)* and the topics in the box.

> Travel and transport   Clothes   Food
> Money   Education and schools   Sports
> Science   Entertainment (TV, films etc.)
> Books   .... (your idea)

A: *I think students will learn from home with computers.*
B: *Yes, I agree, and there might not be any teachers or schools!*

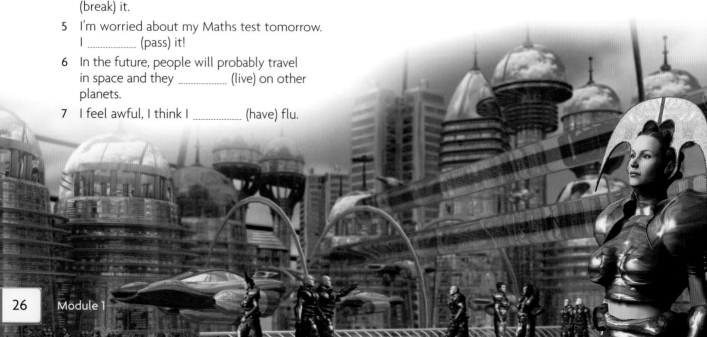

7 Grammar and speaking

First conditional

a Complete these two sentences from the text on page 24. Then complete the rule.

If the temperatures continue to rise, ...
If the ice melts, ...

> **Rule:** Condition clause   Result clause
> *If +* .... simple + ... / *won't*.

b Complete the sentences. Use the correct form of the verbs.

1 If I __*fail*__ (fail) the exam, I __*'ll take*__ (take) it again.
2 If there .... (be) more cars on the road in the future, there .... (be) more pollution.
3 If you .... (see) Jane, ... you .... (give) her my message?
4 If pollution .... (increase), more plants and animals .... (die).
5 I .... (not tell) you my secret if you .... (not come) to Mark's party with me.
6 My parents .... (be) really angry if they .... (see) my bedroom!

c Complete the questions. Use the correct form of the verbs.

1 What __*will*__ you __*do*__ (do) if the weather __*is nice*__ (be) nice this weekend?
2 Where .... you .... (go) if you .... (go) out this weekend?
3 What .... you .... (buy) if you .... (go) shopping this weekend?
4 If you .... (not go) out this evening, what .... you .... (do)?
5 If your teacher .... (not give) you any homework today, what .... you .... (do)?
6 If you .... (phone) a friend tonight, what .... you .... (talk about)?

d Work with a partner. Ask and answer the questions in Exercise 7c.

A: *What will you do if the weather's nice this weekend?*
B: *I'm not sure. I might play football with Marco.*

e Make sentences about the pictures. Use *If + will/won't, might (not)* or *may (not)*.

If the boy doesn't get up now, he'll be late for school.

unless in first conditional sentences

f Look at the examples from the text on page 24. Then complete the rule.

*The problems of climate change won't go away **unless we do something** about the causes.*
***Unless we do something** to stop global warming now, there may be many other dramatic changes in the future.*

> **Rule:** Circle the correct answer.
> **Unless** we do something = If we **do** / If we **don't do** something.

g Match the two parts of the sentences.

1 Unless we leave now   a unless my dad gives me some.
2 We won't understand   b he'll fail his exams.
3 I won't have any money   c if you don't tell anyone.
4 Unless he studies harder   d we'll be late.
5 Nobody will know our secret e unless our teacher explains.

Culture in mind

8 Listen

(a) 🔊 Match the types of energy with the pictures. Write 1–7 in the boxes. Then listen, check and repeat.

> 1 solar energy   2 wind energy   3 nuclear energy
> 4 waves   5 coal   6 oil   7 hydro-electric dam

(b) 🔊 Which of the things in the pictures are forms of *renewable energy*? Which are examples of *non-renewable energy*? Listen to the first part of a radio interview about energy and check your answers.

(c) 🔊 What problems are there with coal, oil and nuclear power? Listen again and check your answers.

ENERGY
Around the World

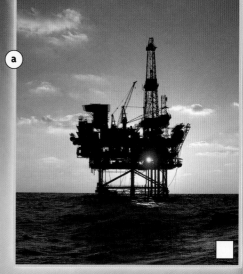

a

b

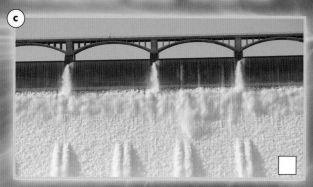

c

d

e

f

g

Country	Austria	Denmark	Finland	France	Germany	Ireland	Italy	Spain	Sweden	UK
Percentage of renewable energy	25%	10%	21.3%	7.1%	2.4%	2.0%	5.5%	5.7%	25.4%	about 1%

d 🔊 Listen to the second part of the radio interview. Tick (✓) the type of energy each country uses.

	Austria	Brazil	France	Sweden	USA
Wind energy					
Solar energy					✓
Wave energy					
Hydro-electric energy					

9 Speak

Look at the information on page 28 about renewable energy in Europe in the year 2000. Which countries had the most renewable energy? Which countries had the least?

Discussion box

Work in pairs or small groups. Discuss these questions together.

1 How important do you think renewable energy is? Why?

2 What kind of renewable energy do you have in your country (if any)?

3 There are also problems with renewable sources of energy. What kinds of problems do you think there are?

10 Write

a Amy wrote an article for her school website. How many ideas does she have for making her town better for teenagers? Read Amy's article below to find the answers.

b Underline the words and phrases Amy uses to introduce each idea in her article. Circle the words and phrases she uses to give her opinion.

c Write a short article for your school website. Say what you think individual people can do to improve the environment in your town or city.

- Use your ideas from the speaking activity on page 25 and some of the vocabulary in the unit.
- Use Amy's article to help you. Use the language you underlined and circled to introduce ideas and give opinions.

d Plan your writing. Here is a possible plan:

1 say where you live and what you think some of the environment problems are

2 say what you think people can do

3 think of a positive ending for your article

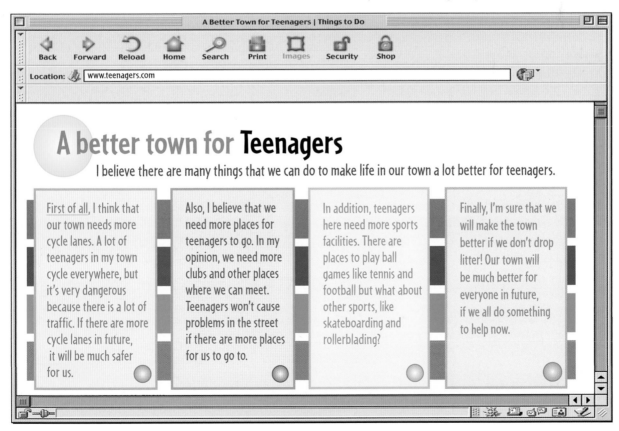

A Better Town for Teenagers | Things to Do

Back Forward Reload Home Search Print Images Security Shop

Location: www.teenagers.com

A better town for **Teenagers**

I believe there are many things that we can do to make life in our town a lot better for teenagers.

First of all, I think that our town needs more cycle lanes. A lot of teenagers in my town cycle everywhere, but it's very dangerous because there is a lot of traffic. If there are more cycle lanes in future, it will be much safer for us.

Also, I believe that we need more places for teenagers to go. In my opinion, we need more clubs and other places where we can meet. Teenagers won't cause problems in the street if there are more places for us to go to.

In addition, teenagers here need more sports facilities. There are places to play ball games like tennis and football but what about other sports, like skateboarding and rollerblading?

Finally, I'm sure that we will make the town better if we don't drop litter! Our town will be much better for everyone in future, if we all do something to help now.

For your portfolio

Module 1 Check your progress

1 Grammar

(a) Complete the sentences. Use the past simple or past continuous form of the verbs.

While I _was walking_ (walk) down the street yesterday, I ¹_____ (see) a friend of mine. He ²_____ (look) in a shop window. I ³_____ (start) to cross the road to say hello to him. While I ⁴_____ (cross) the road, I ⁵_____ (hear) a noise. A bus ⁶_____ (come) in my direction! The bus ⁷_____ (stop) very close to me. I was lucky it ⁸_____ (not hit) me! **[8]**

(b) Complete the sentences. Use the comparative or superlative form of the underlined adjectives.

1 I'm a good player, but Steve is ___better___ than me and Jane is the _____ player in the school!

2 Question 1 was easy. Question 4 was _____ than question 1, and question 6 was the _____ of all.

3 Last night's match was exciting, but Saturday's match was _____ than last night's match, and Sunday's match was the _____ I've ever seen.

4 Yesterday was a bad day for me, but Thursday was _____ than yesterday, and Friday was the _____ day of my life! **[7]**

(c) Complete the sentences. Write the adverbs.

1 They ran home _quickly_ (quick).

2 She looked at me _____ (nervous).

3 My brother speaks French _____ (fluent).

4 The hairdresser cut my hair very _____ (bad).

5 I answered all the questions _____ (easy).

6 Our team played very _____ (good). **[5]**

(d) Complete the sentences. Use the comparative adverbs of the adjectives.

1 I can't understand you. Can you speak _more clearly_ (clear) please?

2 I did yesterday's test _____ (easy) than the test last month.

3 I think Americans speak _____ (fast) than English people.

4 My mum always gets up _____ (early) than me.

5 I played well, but Mike won because he played _____ (good) than me.

6 Alison has to walk _____ (far) than me to get to the town centre. **[5]**

(e) Complete the sentences with 'll/will or won't.

1 Do you think it _'ll rain_ (rain) tomorrow?

2 I'm really tired so I think I _____ (go) to bed early tonight.

3 I'm sure Andy _____ (not come) to the party on Saturday, he's ill.

4 When I leave school, I think I _____ (try) to get a job in the USA.

5 Tell me your secret! I promise I _____ (not tell) anyone.

6 Ask James for some help. I'm sure he _____ (know) the answer. **[5]**

(f) Rewrite the sentences. Use might or might not.

1 Perhaps I'll stay at home this weekend.
I _might stay_ at home this weekend.

2 Joanne isn't at home, maybe she's in town.
Joanne isn't at home, she _____ in town.

3 Perhaps I won't go to Spain this summer.
I _____ to Spain this summer.

4 Maybe my parents will give me some new trainers for my birthday.
My parents _____ me some new trainers for my birthday.

5 Perhaps we'll see you tomorrow.
We _____ you tomorrow. **[4]**

(g) Complete the sentences with the correct forms of the verbs.

1 If Tom _invites_ (invite) me, _I'll go_ (go) to the party.

2 If I _____ (work) hard, my parents _____ (give) me some extra money.

3 I _____ (phone) Mike if he _____ (not arrive) before 10 o'clock.

4 If you _____ (speak) very fast, they _____ (not understand) you.

5 If Marco _____ (phone) tonight, _____ you _____ (tell) him I'm at Sally's house?

6 My parents _____ (not know) if you _____ (not tell) them. **[5]**

2 Vocabulary

(a) Put the letters in order to find the adjectives and write them next to their opposites.

| ~~ogod~~ udifticfl   smeys   yonsi   smil |
| lows   holaslw |

1	bad	_good_	5	tidy	....
2	fast	....	6	quiet	....
3	deep	....	7	easy	....
4	fat	....			

| 6 |

(b) Complete the sentences. Use the correct form of the verb *get* and one of the words in the box.

| home   a surprise   good ideas |
| the answer   old   ~~wet~~ |

1 It rained very hard last Saturday when I was in town, and I _got_ very _wet_ .

2 Our dog can't walk very well because he's .... very .... now.

3 I .... yesterday. My uncle sent me some money!

4 The party was great, and I didn't .... until midnight!

5 My brother says he .... when he daydreams.

6 I love Maths, and I'm always happy when I ....

| 5 |

(c) Complete sentences 1–9 and fill in the puzzle with words about the environment. What's the mystery word?

```
1    D |   |   | P |   |
2      P |   |   |   |   |
3          |   |   | B |   | L |   |
4  R |   |   |   |   | E |   |
5            |   | B |   |   |   |   |
6  W |   |   |   |   |
7            |   | K |   |   |
8            |   |   |   | T |   |
9  |   |   |   |   | N |   |   |
```

1 Please don't .... litter on the floor.

2 If we don't do something now, the ice at the .... will melt.

3 Temperatures around the world are rising every year. This is called .... warming.

4 You can .... glass, but you can't .... plastic.

5 Please put your .... in the bin over there.

6 Please turn off the TV. Don't .... electricity!

7 There's a lot of litter here on the street – let's .... it up.

8 There's a very large rain............... in the Amazon.

9 My bike's very dirty, so I'm going to .... it.

| 9 |

3 Everyday English

Complete the dialogue with the words in the box.

| actually   hold on   I'm off   stop it |
| ~~round here~~   too right |

Paul: I really don't like our town – there's nothing to do ¹ _round here_!

Sandra: ² ....! It's a really boring place, isn't it?

Josh: Do you think so? ³ ...., I think there's lots to do here.

Sandra: How do you know? You never go out!

Josh: ⁴ ...., Sandra!

Paul: Isn't there a new club in Bridge Street?

Sandra: ⁵ .... a minute – I didn't know there's a new club there.

Paul: Really? Well listen, Sandra, let's go there together on Friday.

Josh: You two are crazy! Look, ⁶ .... now, see you tomorrow.

| 5 |

How did you do?

Tick (✓) a box for each section.

Total score	☺ Very good	☻ OK	☹ Not very good
64			
Grammar	30 – 39	25 – 29	less than 25
Vocabulary	16 – 20	11 – 15	less than 11
Everyday English	4 – 5	3	less than 3

Module 2
Different lives

YOU WILL LEARN ABOUT ...

- Canada and the USA ....
- A coming of age ceremony on a Pacific island ....
- Minimum age limits around the world ....
- A Japanese ceremony ....
- Clown doctors ....
- A stuntwoman ....
- Hollywood film stars and their lifestyles ....

 Can you match each photo with a topic?

YOU WILL LEARN HOW TO ...

Speak
- Discuss answers to a quiz
- Check information
- Describe recently completed activities
- Talk about what you are (not) allowed to do
- Discuss minimum age limits
- Talk about things that make you laugh
- Talk about things you enjoy / don't like
- Talk about films
- Discuss the advantages and disadvantages of fame

Write
- An email about a holiday
- A magazine article about a special day
- An email describing how you enjoy yourself
- A film review

Read
- A quiz about Canada and the USA
- An article about a young poet
- A poem
- An article about a coming of age ceremony
- A quiz about minimum ages around the world
- An interview with a clown doctor
- A questionnaire about having fun
- An article about a stuntwoman
- Short film reviews and descriptions of people
- A web page about Hollywood film stars

Listen
- A dialogue about Canada and the USA
- A dialogue about a trip to New York
- A story about a legend
- A dialogue about minimum age limits
- An interview with a clown doctor
- A song
- A dialogue about films
- A conversation about a film star

Use grammar

Can you match the names of the grammar points with the examples?

Question tags	Thousands of trees **are cut down** every day.
Present perfect + *just*	**Have you done** the washing up **yet**?
Present perfect + *already/yet*	**I've lived** here **since** I was 10.
Present simple passive	I **enjoy cycling**, so I've **decided to buy** a new bike.
let / be allowed to	You live round here, **don't you**?
Present perfect + *for/since*	My parents never **let me** stay up late.
Verbs + *ing* or infinitive	**I've just finished** my exams.

Use vocabulary

Can you think of two more examples for each topic?

British/American English	Describing age	Verb/noun pairs	Film
flat/apartment	middle-aged	have a drink	director
lorry/truck	a child	make a mistake	comedy
....	....	....	....
....	....	....	....

5 Canada and the USA

✳ Question tags
✳ Present perfect simple, *just/already/yet*
✳ Vocabulary: North American and British English

1 Read and listen

(a) What do you know about Canada and the USA? Do the quiz. For each question, (circle) one answer, a, b or c.

(b) 🔊 Now listen to a Canadian girl, Laura, talking to her English friend, Tony, and check your answers to the quiz.

How much do you know about CANADA AND THE USA?

Geography

1 What's the capital of the USA?
a New York   b Washington, DC   c San Francisco

2 What's the capital of Canada?
a Montreal   b Toronto   c Ottawa

3 Canada is the .... country in the world.
a largest   b second largest   c third largest

4 How many states are there in the USA?
a 50   b 49   c 52

Language and people

5 Which country has a bigger population than Canada?
a Italy   b Australia   c Greece

6 French and English are the two official languages in Canada. How many people speak French as their first language?
a about 50% of the population
b about 30% of the population
c about 10% of the population

7 Which city has the largest population of Chinese people outside China?
a New York, USA   b San Francisco, USA   c Vancouver, Canada

8 The population of the USA is about 280 million. How many people speak Spanish as their <u>first</u> language?
a about 10 million   b about 28 million   c about 55 million

9 What's the most popular sport in Canada?
a football   b ice hockey   c baseball

10 What's the most popular sport in the USA?
a ice hockey   b baseball   c American football

2 Grammar

Question tags

a 🔊 Complete these sentences from the dialogue in Exercise 1b. Then listen to the first part of Laura and Tony's conversation again and check your answers.

1 You're from Canada, __aren't__ you?
2 You live in the USA, _____ you?
3 You can tell me about the USA and Canada, _____ you?
4 New York's the capital of the USA, _____ it?
5 Toronto isn't the capital of Canada, _____ it?
6 You don't know much about Canada, _____ you?

b All the questions in Exercise 2a have 'tags' at the end. 'Tags' are short questions which we use to check facts or make conversation. Complete the rule.

> **Rule:**
> - With positive statements, we usually use a _____ question tag. With negative statements, we usually use a _____ question tag.
> - With the verb *to be*, modal verbs (*can, must, should, will, might*), *have got* (present tense) and the present perfect tense, repeat the verb in the tag.
> - With all other verbs, use _____ / *does* (present simple) or _____ / *didn't* (past simple).

c Match the statements and the tags. Write the numbers in the boxes.

1 He's American,	isn't it?	☐
2 She doesn't like me,	have you?	☐
3 She can come with us,	aren't they?	☐
4 They're not from Canada,	do you?	☐
5 They're from the USA,	will she?	☐
6 Your favourite food is pasta,	does she?	☐
7 She won't be at the party,	can't she?	☐
8 You don't know Clare,	isn't he?	1
9 You've been to Italy,	are they?	☐
10 You haven't got a brother,	haven't you?	☐

d Write the question tags.

1 He saw us, __didn't he__ ?
2 They don't live here, _____ ?
3 She likes chocolate, _____ ?
4 You weren't at the party, _____ ?
5 They went to New York, _____ ?
6 She goes to your school, _____ ?
7 They didn't enjoy the film, _____ ?
8 She lived in Toronto, _____ ?

3 Pronunciation

Intonation in question tags

🔊 Turn to page 120.

4 Speak

a Work in groups of four. Ask each other these questions. Don't write the answers!

- What time do you usually get up on Sunday?
- What do you usually eat for breakfast?
- What did you have for breakfast this morning?
- What's your favourite colour?
- How often do you go shopping?
- Have you ever been to the USA?

b Now try to remember your friends' answers. Use question tags.

Anna, you usually get up at 10 o'clock on Sunday, don't you?

c Work with a partner. Use the words below to make sentences about him/her that you think are true. Then add tags to make them into questions to ask your partner.

You don't like Chinese food, do you?

- Chinese food
- fifteen years old
- football
- a big house
- Maths
- English
- brother
- swim

5 Read

(a) Linda Ho has won a prize in a competition. What kind of competition is it? When did Linda get her idea? What does she want to do in the future? Read the newspaper article to find the answers.

$1,000 FOR YOUNG VANCOUVER POET

Sixteen-year-old Linda Ho from Richmond, Vancouver has won the British Columbia 'Young Poet of the Year' competition, with her poem *Whale Song*. Linda, from Steveston High School, takes home a prize of $1,000.

Linda has already written about 30 poems, but she has never entered a competition before now. 'It was a big surprise for me,' she says. 'I didn't expect to win.'

Linda says that she thought of the poem when she came out of an elevator and saw a painting of a whale on a wall. 'But sometimes I get ideas for poems when I'm walking on the sidewalk, or when I'm on the subway,' she says.

Linda has already decided how to spend the prize money. 'A web camera for my computer, and some books by my favorite poets.' Linda has just done her school-leaving examinations, and she hopes to go to university to study Marine Biology. 'I haven't decided about a career yet,' says Linda. 'But I'd like to work in something to do with the sea, for sure.'

Linda also wants to keep writing poetry. 'I've won one competition, it would be nice to win another one!'

(b) 🔊 Read and listen to Linda's prize-winning poem. What is it about? Do you like it? Why / Why not?

6 Vocabulary

British vs. North American English

🔊 Put the words in the correct spaces. Then listen to another conversation with Tony and Laura and check your answers.

> pavement – sidewalk
> pants – trousers
> elevator – lift
> garbage – rubbish
> underground – subway
> flat – apartment

	Britain	North America
(a)	....	....
(b)	....	....
(c)	....	....
(d)	....	....
(e)	....	....
(f)	....	....

WHALE SONG

Have you seen the whales yet?
  Have you heard their song?

A quiet day. A boat. A whale.
  A sea of blood and death.
A fight, a storm, their work is done.
  Twelve men are out of breath.

'A thousand bucks for each of us.
  It's time to celebrate.
The biggest one we've ever caught –
  We've never felt so great!'

Have you heard the whale song?
  Have you felt the pain?

7 Grammar

Present perfect simple, *already* and *yet*

a Look at the examples. <u>Underline</u> other examples of the present perfect simple in the article on page 36. Then complete the rule.

Linda has already decided how to spend the prize money. I haven't decided about a career yet.

> **Rule:**
> - Form the present perfect simple with the verb _____ and the _____ form of the main verb.
> - Use *yet* in questions and _____ sentences. Use *already* in positive sentences.
> - Use *already* between *have* and the _____ _____ . Use _____ at the end of the sentence or question.

b Write the statements and questions. Use the present perfect and *yet* or *already*.

1 A: John! *Have you done your homework yet?* _____
   (you / do your homework?)

   B: Nearly, Dad. _____
   (I / finish the Maths, but / not start the History.)

2 A: I love 'All in one' but _____
   (I / not buy their new CD.)

   B: Don't buy it! _____
   (I / buy it for you!)

3 A: _____
   (Maria / do the shopping?)

   B: Yes and _____
   (she / buy everything for the party.)

4 A: _____
   (Sam and Tom / see the film?)

   B: Yes and _____
   (they / read the book, too.)

8 Listen and speak

a 🔊 Steve is on holiday in New York. Listen to his conversation with Gill. Tick (✓) the things he has already done. Put a cross (✗) next to the things he hasn't done yet.

1 see the Empire State Building ☐
2 have a ride in a yellow cab ☐
3 travel on the subway ☐
4 been to the Hard Rock Café ☐
5 watch a baseball game ☐
6 eat an American hamburger ☐

b Now check your answers with a partner. Ask and answer questions.

A: *Has he seen the Empire State Building yet?*
B: *Yes, he has.*

9 Grammar

Present perfect with *just*

a Look at the example. Then complete the rule.

Linda has just done her school-leaving examinations.

> **Rule:** We often use _____ in positive sentences with the present perfect when we want to say that an action happened a very short time ago.

b Use the words to make two sentences about each picture. Use the present perfect with *just* and *yet*.

He's just got a letter, but he hasn't opened it yet.

get a letter / open

do the shopping / do the cooking

go to bed / switch off light

make breakfast / eat

buy new DVD / watch

score goal / win

You said 6.30, didn't you?

10 Read and listen

a 🔊 Who are the three people in the first photo? Who arrives later?
How does Amy feel? Why, do you think? Read, listen and check your answers.

Dave: So, it looks like we have a band. The four of us.

Joanne: That's right. But where's our little singer ... what's her name?

Dave: Amy. She hasn't arrived yet – but she'll be here soon.

Joanne: Well, we can start without her, can't we?

Matt: Sure, why not? Dave?

Dave: Er ... OK. Joanne, you sing, all right?

Joanne: Sure. What's the first number?

Matt: It's 'Gone Away' by Anna Craven.

Joanne: Great! Off we go. One, two, three, four ...

A few minutes later

Dave: Wow, Joanne. That was wicked!

Matt: Yeah, nice one.

Amy: Hi Dave!

Dave: Amy. You're late.

Amy: What do you mean? You said 6.30, didn't you?

Dave: No I didn't, I said six o'clock. We've already done one song.

Matt: Hi Amy, I'm Matt. This is Joanne.

Amy: Oh, hello Matt. Hello, Joanne ...

Joanne: Hi. So, Dave – shall I do the next song?

Dave: Well, Amy usually ...

Amy: Oh, it's OK, you can do the next one, Joanne. I'd like to hear you.

b Mark the statements *T* (true) or *F* (false).

1 Joanne remembers Amy's name.
2 The three of them decide to wait until Amy arrives.
3 The first song is called *Go Away*.
4 Dave and Matt think Joanne's singing was very good.
5 Amy and Dave don't agree about the time of the rehearsal.
6 Joanne doesn't reply to Amy.

11 Everyday English

a Find expressions 1–4 from the story. Who says them? Match them with definitions a–d.

1 Sure.   a let's start
2 Off we go.   b really good
3 Nice one.   c yes, OK
4 Wicked!   d you did that
                      very well

b Complete the sentences with the <u>underlined</u> words from Exercise 11a.

1 Sue: Have you seen the new Hugh Grant film yet?
   Sam: Yes, I have. I thought it was _____ !

2 Dad: OK. Is everybody in the car? Yes? OK, then – _____ !

3 Tom: Let's go to the cinema tonight.
   Lynn: _____ , that's a good idea.

4 Ella: I got 100% in my English test!
   Anne: _____ ! What did you parents say?

12 Write

a Read the email from Sarah to Mark. Answer these questions.

1 Which cities has Sarah already visited?
2 Where did she go yesterday, and what did she think of it?
3 Has she visited the Golden Gate Bridge yet?
4 Has she been on a tram yet?
5 What has she bought as a present for Mark?

| Get Msg | Write Msg | Reply | File | Delete | Stop | Print |

Hi Mark!
How are things with you? Thanks for your email – I got it yesterday. So, here I am on holiday in California – and I'm in an Internet café in San Francisco, writing to you!

We're having a great time. We've already been to San Diego and Los Angeles – San Francisco is the last city on our holiday (they say 'vacation' here).

It's a great place and the weather's beautiful. We've already done lots of things! Yesterday we went to Alcatraz prison, on an island – really interesting! We haven't visited the Golden Gate Bridge yet, but of course I've seen it! Oh, but we've already travelled on one of the streetcars (trams) here – it was wicked!

Well, it's time for dinner – we're going to a Mexican restaurant tonight, I can't wait!

Hope everything's OK with you – write to me again soon, OK?
Love,
Sarah
PS – I've already bought a present for you – a San Francisco Giants baseball cap! Hope you like it!

b Now answer these questions.

1 How does Sarah begin her email?
2 How does she finish the email?
3 Sarah thinks of something more to say after she writes her name; how does she begin this?

c Imagine you are on holiday in a city. Choose one of the cities in the box (or a different city).

New York   Rome   London   Rio de Janeiro   Paris

Write a similar email to an English-speaking friend. Tell him/her what you have and haven't done. Use Sarah's email to help you.

6

Growing up

* Present simple passive
* *let / be allowed to*
* Vocabulary: describing a person's age

1 Read and listen

(a) Where are the people in the pictures from? What do you think they are doing? Read the text quickly and check your ideas.

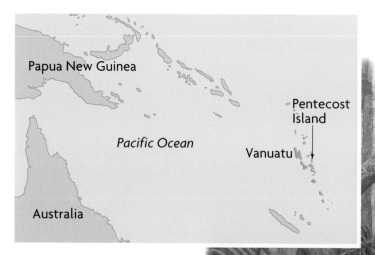

Papua New Guinea

Pacific Ocean

Pentecost Island

Vanuatu

Australia

(b) 🔊 Read the text again and listen. Answer the questions.

1. How tall is the bamboo tower?
2. Why do the boys go into the forest?
3. What do the boys do with the lianas?
4. What idea did the British tourists have, after they watched the ceremony?

(c) Do you think N'gol is more dangerous than bungee jumping? Why / Why not?

from TEENAGER to ADULT

When does a teenager become an adult? In many countries, you become an adult on your eighteenth birthday, but to become an adult in Pentecost, boys have to do something special. Pentecost is a small island in the Pacific Ocean, and every year in April and May, an important ceremony is held there. The ceremony is called N'gol.

First, bamboo trees are cut down and a bamboo tower, about 25 metres high, is built. A platform of leaves and branches is made, and this is put at the top of the bamboo tower.

The boys then go into the forest to find lianas. Each boy must find, cut and measure his own liana because the older men do not help him. The boy climbs to the top of the tower, where he ties one end of the liana to the tower and the other end to his foot. Then he jumps from the top of the tower. If the liana breaks, or if it is too long, the boy might die. A boy cannot become a man until he has jumped from the tower.

Sometimes, the N'gol ceremony is watched by tourists. A few years ago, a group of British people watched it, and it gave them the idea for a new sport called bungee jumping.

2 Grammar

Present simple passive

a We form the present simple passive with the verb *be* + the past participle of the main verb. Look at the examples.

*First, bamboo trees **are cut** down ...*   *... a bamboo tower ... **is built** ...*

b <u>Underline</u> other examples of the present simple passive in the text on page 40. Then read the rule and complete the table.

> **Rule:** Use the passive when it isn't important who does the action, or when we don't know who does it.

Positive	Negative	Question	Short answer
A liana **is** used.	A rope .... (is not) used.	.... a rope **used**?	Yes, it ....
Lianas .... **used**.	Ropes .... (are not) used.	.... ropes **used**?	No, they ....

c Complete the sentences with the present simple passive form of the verbs. Check with the list of irregular verbs on page 124.

1 Millions of pizzas _are eaten_ (eat) in the world every year.
2 How many emails .... (write) every day?
3 Coca-Cola .... (sell) in almost every country in the world.
4 Rice .... (not grow) in England, but it .... (grow) in Spain.
5 .... most emails .... (send) from home computers?
6 Ferrari cars .... (make) in Italy.

d Rewrite the sentences. Use the present simple passive.

1 People make jeans in the USA.
   Jeans are made in the USA .
2 Someone picks up litter every morning.
   Litter ....
3 People cut down a lot of trees every year.
   A lot ....
4 People waste too much water.
   Too much ....
5 Postal workers deliver thousands of letters.
   Thousands ....
6 Do they make successful films in Hollywood?
   Are .... ?
7 Do they grow coffee in Kenya?
   Is .... ?

e Look at the pictures. Make sentences about the opening ceremony of the Olympic Games.

1 torch / take / to the Olympic city
2 flag / carry / into the stadium
3 flame / light / with the torch
4 Games / open / with a speech

3 Listen and speak

a) These pictures tell the story of how the N'gol ceremony began, but they are in the wrong order. Work with a partner and try to guess the correct order. Write 1–8 in the boxes.

b) 🔊 Listen to the story and check your answers.

4 Vocabulary

Describing a person's age

a) 🔊 Match the words with the photos. Write 1–6 in the boxes. Then listen, check and repeat.

> 1 a young adult   2 a child   3 a teenager   4 a baby   5 a toddler   6 a pensioner

b) Complete the sentences with your own ideas.

1 You're a baby until you are _____ years old.
2 You're a toddler from the age of _____ to _____ .
3 I think you're a child until you are _____ years old.
4 You're a teenager from the age of _____ to _____ .
5 I think you become an adult when you are _____ years old.
6 In my country, you become a pensioner when you are _____ years old.

c) How old is someone who is *middle-aged*, do you think? How old is someone who is *elderly*? How do you say *elderly* and *middle-aged* in your language?

5 Grammar

let / be allowed to

a 🔊 Read and listen to the dialogue. Then answer the questions.

Melissa: Hey Andy – what's wrong?

Andy: I really want to go to the music festival in Leeds next weekend – but I'm not allowed to go. My parents say I'm too young.

Melissa: Oh, that's terrible! I had the same problem last month – my dad didn't let me go to the Liverpool match.

Andy: Actually, my parents usually let me do things. I'm allowed to stay out until midnight at weekends.

Melissa: Really? That's cool! My dad never lets me do *anything*. Sometimes I think school's better than home – at least we're allowed to breathe at school!

Andy: Does your dad let you stay up late to watch TV?

Melissa: Well, yes, sometimes – but only if I've done all my homework!

1 Where does Andy want to go?
2 Why can't he go there?
3 Why didn't Melissa go to the match last month?
4 What does Andy say about his parents and weekends?
5 What does Melissa's dad sometimes let her do?

b Look at the examples.

*… my Dad **didn't let me go** to the match.*
*I'm **allowed to stay** out until midnight.*

Underline other examples of *let* and *be allowed to* in Exercise 5a. Then complete the rule.

> **Rule:**
> * Use .... to say you do or don't have permission to do something.
> * Use .... to say that someone gives or doesn't give you permission to do something.
> * Both *let* and *be allowed to* are followed by the infinitive: *I'm not allowed to **go**. My dad didn't let me **go**.*
> * With *let*, use *let* + person + infinitive without *to*: *Does he let you stay up?*

c Complete the sentences with the correct form of *be allowed to*.

1 Look at the sign, Dad! We *aren't allowed to* turn right here.
2 Sorry, you .... take photos in the museum.
3 There's a river in our town, but we .... swim in it.
4 We can take our bikes into the park, Steve – you .... cycle there.
5 My dad smokes but he .... smoke at home.
6 .... I .... park my car here?

d Write the sentences using *let (someone) do.*

1 I don't listen to music after midnight – my parents say no. *My parents don't let me listen to music after midnight* .
2 I watch the late-night movie on Fridays – my parents say I can. ....
3 My brother doesn't use my computer – I say no. ....
4 We never run in the corridors at my school – the teachers say no. ....
5 We don't wear trainers to school – the principal says no. ....
6 I drive our car sometimes – my dad says it's OK! ....

e What are you (not) allowed to do at your school? In your home? Make a list. Then talk to other people in your class.

A: *Are you allowed to stay up late at weekends?*
B: *Yes, I am. Do your parents …*

6 Pronunciation

/aʊ/ allowed

🔊 Turn to page 120.

Culture in mind

7 Read

Read the magazine page and do the quiz.
Then work with a partner and compare your answers.

Call yourself an adult?

Are you desperately waiting to be eighteen, so you can call yourself 'an adult'? OK. No problem! You probably think that teenagers in <u>every</u> country are doing the same thing – but you are wrong! Age limits vary all around the world. Try our quiz and you might get some surprises!

BRITAIN

1. You're allowed to drive a car from the age of:
   a 16   b 17   c 18

2. You are allowed to get married when you are:
   a 16   b 17   c 18

3. But you can't vote until you are:
   a 17   b 18   c 21

THE USA

4. You're usually allowed to vote from the age of:
   a 16   b 17   c 18

5. In most American states, you're allowed to drive a car from the age of:
   a 16   b 17   c 18

6. In New York, you're allowed to get married from the age of:
   a 16   b 17   c 18

7. But in California, you can only get married from the age of:
   a 16   b 17   c 18

THE FAR EAST

8. In China, women can get married from the age of … , and men from the age of … :
   a 20/22   b 19/21   c 18/20

9. And in Japan, you're allowed to get married from the age of … if you're a girl, and … if you're a boy!
   a 14/17   b 16/18   c 15/19

10. In Japan, people can vote when they are:
    a 18   b 20   c 21

8 Listen

🔊 Listen to Mandy and Alex discussing the quiz on page 44. Check your answers.

Discussion box

Work in pairs or small groups. Discuss these questions together.

1 What are the minimum age limits in your country for:
  ● getting married?
  ● driving a car?
  ● voting?

2 What other minimum age limits are there in your country?

3 What do you think of the minimum age limits in your country?

9 Write

(a) Eri has written an article for her English school magazine about a Japanese ceremony. What is the ceremony for? Read her article to find the answer.

(b) Match the questions with the paragraphs. Write A, B and C in the boxes.

1 What is *Seijin No Hi*? ☐

2 What happens during the ceremony? ☐

3 How do the girls prepare for the ceremony? ☐

(c) Write a magazine article about how you celebrate a special day in your country. Use Eri's article to help you.

SEIJIN NO HI

Coming of Age in *Japan*

A In Japan, young people come of age when they are 20. This event is celebrated in most areas of Japan with a special ceremony, called *Seijin No Hi* or Coming of Age. On this important day in January, young people who are from the same area and were all in the same school year, go together to their local town hall, where the ceremony is held.

B The day often starts early for the girls, because they have to dress up for the ceremony. They wear a traditional Japanese dress (or kimono). They are extremely expensive, so most girls have to hire or borrow one. Because the dress is very difficult to put on, some girls go to a special place where other women help them. They sometimes spend up to three hours getting dressed and doing their hair and make-up. Most boys wear suits, but some wear a traditional Japanese kimono for men.

C When they are ready, the young people are photographed with their families. All the girls and boys then go to the local town hall or government office, where more photos are taken. In the hall, they listen to long speeches and sometimes sing songs. They are then given a special certificate or present from the local government. The boys and girls, now men and women, then go outside, where many more photos are taken. Finally, they leave and go out to celebrate together.

For your portfolio

7

Have a laugh!

* Present perfect simple, *for* vs. *since*
* Vocabulary: verb and noun pairs

1 Read and listen

a The dialogue is a radio interview with a clown doctor called Fran Mason.
Why do you think she's in the hospital? Read her answers and check your ideas.

Interview with a Clown Doctor

Interviewer: Good morning to all our listeners. This morning I'm talking to Fran Mason, who's a clown doctor. Fran, what is a clown doctor?

Fran: Well, we aren't really doctors, we're clowns. But we pretend to be doctors. We go to children's hospitals and do all kinds of crazy things to make the sick children laugh.

Interviewer:
a _____ ?

Fran: I wear a doctor's white coat and I pretend to examine a little boy or girl, for example, but then I make funny faces. They love it!

Interviewer:
b _____ ?

Fran: Oh, yes. But we don't give the children medicine. We think *laughter* is the best medicine. It's very important for them to laugh, smile and enjoy themselves.

Interviewer:
c _____ ?

Fran: I've been a clown doctor for three years, and before I became a clown doctor I was a teacher for ten years. You see, I really enjoy working with children but I wanted to do something a bit different.

Interviewer:
d _____ ?

Fran: I've worked here since last year. I worked as a clown doctor for a year in Australia, and then

I came to London last December, for Christmas. I go to six different hospitals in London and I see a lot of kids, and teenagers too.

Interviewer:
e _____ ?

Fran: Well, the best thing is seeing the children laugh. But I also love working with the doctors and nurses. Lots of them say they laugh too, when they see the children having fun.

Interviewer: I think you do really wonderful work, Fran. Thanks and good luck.

b 🔊 Put questions 1–5 in the correct places in the interview. Then listen and check.

1 And how long have you worked in London?
2 What do you enjoy most about the work you do?
3 Does it help the children to get better?
4 How long have you been a clown doctor?
5 What do you do to make them laugh?

c Answer the questions.

1 Do clown doctors give children medicine?
2 How does Fran make the children laugh?
3 Why does she enjoy her job?

d Fran says: 'We think laughter is the best medicine.' Do you agree?

2 Grammar
Present perfect simple

a Look at the example. Then answer the question and complete the rule.

I've been a clown doctor for three years.

Is Fran a clown doctor now?

> **Rule:** Use the ___ ___ ___ for things that started in the past and continue to the present (now).

b Underline other examples of the present perfect simple in the interview.

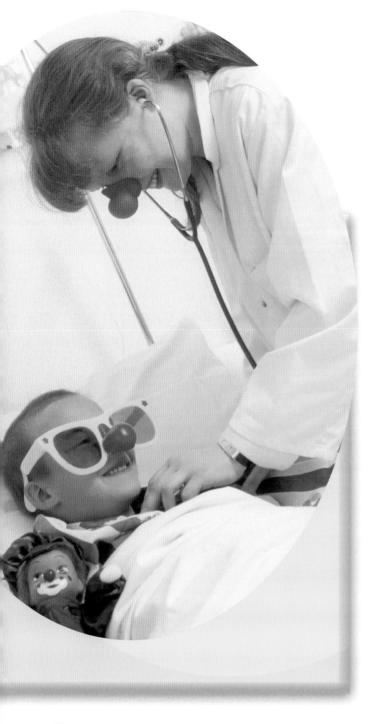

for vs. *since*

d Look at the examples.

*How long **have you been** a clown doctor?*
***For** three years.*

*And how long **have you worked** in London?*
***Since** last year.*

When do we use *for* and when do we use *since*? Write the words in two lists.

> ~~yesterday~~   ~~a week~~   Christmas   two years
> an hour   1999   Saturday   a month
> I was 11   last weekend   a long time   days

for _____*a week*_____   since _____*yesterday*_____

e Make as many correct sentences as you can with the words in the table.

I've studied English		I was 11 years old.
They've been married		20 years.
John has had his bicycle	for	last Christmas.
I haven't seen Mark		two weeks.
We've lived here	since	2001.
Maria hasn't spoken to John		ages.
		yesterday.

f Re-write these sentences. Use *for* or *since* and the correct form of the verb.

1 I really like Sara. I *'ve known* (know) her __*since*__ I was ten.
2 You _____ (have) a cold _____ two weeks, so I think you should go to the doctor.
3 My mum's really good at French. She _____ (study) it _____ years.
4 I don't know where Peter is. I _____ (not see) him _____ this morning.
5 We _____ (not be) to the cinema _____ a long time. Why don't we go this weekend?
6 My friend usually writes every week, but she _____ (not write) to me _____ last month.

c Complete the sentences with the present perfect form of the verbs.

1 I *'ve had* (have) my bicycle for two years and it's great!
2 Fran _____ (work) in hospitals for three years.
3 _____ Maria _____ (live) here for a long time?
4 How long _____ your parents _____ (be) married?
5 Tomek _____ (not study) English for a long time.
6 Diana and Jenny _____ (be) friends since 1999.
7 We _____ (not have) our dog for very long. We bought him four months ago.
8 _____ Fran _____ (see) a lot of children this morning?

3 Pronunciation

have, has and *for*

🔊 Turn to page 120.

4 Speak and read

a) Work with a partner. Ask and answer the questions in the present perfect. Use *for* and *since* in your answers. How long have you …

- (know) your best friend?
- (be) at this school?
- (have) your dog/computer/bike?
- (play) the piano/violin?
- (study) English?
- (live) in this town?

A: *How long have you known your best friend?*
B: *For five years. / Since I was nine years old.*

b) Work with a partner. Ask the questions in the questionnaire and tick (✓) your partner's answers. Use the 'Score for answers' to add up the score. Then turn to page 122 and tell your partner the result.

Are you fun to be with?

1 It's your birthday. Your friends have given you a present, but when you open it there's nothing inside. Do you:

a get angry and tell your friends it was a stupid joke?

b think it was a good joke and laugh about it with your friends?

c feel hurt, but try to laugh about it?

2 You and your friend have decided to meet at four o'clock outside your favourite café. You've waited for more than half an hour and finally your friend arrives. She made a mistake and went to the wrong café. What do you say?

a 'Where have you been? I've been here since four o'clock! I'm going home now.'

b 'Never mind, let's go inside and have a coffee.'

c 'I never want to see you again!'

3 You've bought some new clothes. You think they look good, but when your friends see you wearing them, they laugh and make fun of you. Do you:

a feel angry and hurt and decide to take the clothes back to the shop?

b laugh with your friends but keep the clothes?

c smile, because you don't want to show them that you're hurt?

4 It's Saturday and you haven't been out since last week. You're planning to go to your friend's party in the evening, but then your friend phones and tells you there is no party, because he is ill. Do you:

a think it's no big deal because you can always have fun somewhere else?

b feel angry. You've waited all week to go out, and now what will you do?

c tell your friend you're sorry, and try to make him smile again?

5 You are with a group of friends and somebody is telling a joke. You've heard the joke before. Do you:

a say you've already heard the joke and you don't want to hear it again?

b listen to the joke without laughing?

c listen to the joke and have a good laugh with the others?

6 Your friend has invited you to her fancy dress party and you've decided to dress up as a chicken. You think you look funny, but when you arrive at the party no one is wearing fancy dress except you! Your friend has played another practical joke on you. Do you:

a stay at the party and have a good time – it's OK to make a fool of yourself sometimes?

b think it's funny, but go home and change your clothes, then come back to the party?

c feel very angry with your friend and go home straight away?

Score for answers: 1 a: 2 b: 6 c: 4   **2** a: 2 b: 6 c: 0   **3** a: 2 b: 6 c: 4   **4** a: 4 b: 2 c: 6   **5** a: 2 b: 4 c: 6   **6** a: 6 b: 4 c: 0

5 Vocabulary

Verb and noun pairs

a) Write the words from the box next to the verbs. Use the texts on pages 46 and 48 to help you.

> fun   funny faces   fun of someone   a good time
> a fool of yourself   a mistake   a drink
> someone laugh/smile   ~~a (good) laugh~~

have   *a (good) laugh* ....

....

....

make   ....

....

....

b) Complete the sentences. Use the correct form of the verbs in Exercise 5a.

1   When I speak English, I'm afraid I might *make a fool of myself* because I often .... mistakes.

2   It's very important to .... a good laugh.

3   Alan .... everyone laugh in class yesterday, because he .... a funny face.

4   I love .... fun with my friends at weekends. We always .... a good time when we go out.

5   You shouldn't .... fun of other people and laugh at them.

6   Yesterday I met my friend in town. We went shopping, then .... a coffee at my house.

6 Listen

a) Look at the title of the song. How do you say 'Don't worry' in your language?

b) Before you listen, make sure you understand the words in the box.

> landlord   rent   frown   cash   style

c) Match the rhyming pairs. Then fill in the spaces in the song with words 1–5.

1   smile   a   double
2   trouble   b   note
3   down   c   style
4   wrote   d   head
5   bed   e   frown

d) 🔊 Listen to the song and check your answers.

e) Many people say this is a happy song. Does it make you happy? What kind of music do you listen to when you want to have fun?

Don't Worry, Be Happy
by Bobby McFerrin

Here's a little song I [1]...............
You might want to sing it note for note
Don't worry, be happy
In every life we have some [2]...............
When you worry you make it double
Don't worry, be happy
Don't worry, be happy now
Don't worry, be happy (*repeat*)

Ain't got no place to lay your head
Somebody came and took your [3]...............
Don't worry, be happy

The landlord say your rent is late
He may have to litigate
Don't worry, be happy
(Look at me, I'm happy)
Don't worry, be happy
(I give you my phone number, when you worry, call me, I make you happy)
Don't worry, be happy

Ain't got no cash, ain't got no style
Ain't got no girl to make you [4]...............
But don't worry, be happy
'Cause when you worry, your face will frown
And that will bring everybody [5]...............
So don't worry, be happy
Don't worry, be happy now
Don't worry, be happy (*repeat*)

Who's going to sing?

7 Read and listen

a 🔊 Where are Amy and Dave? What are they talking about?
Read, listen and check your answers.

Dave: Shall we have another cup of coffee before we go to the cinema?

Amy: No thanks. Listen, Dave, we haven't talked about the band since the last rehearsal, and I think we need to talk about things.

Dave: What things?

Amy: Well, you know – who's going to sing in the contest?

Dave: Oh, that. Yeah, well, I talked to Matt last night. We both think Joanne's really good.

Amy: Do you mean you don't want me as the singer any more?

Dave: No, Amy, I don't mean that. But we have to do two numbers in the contest, right?

Amy: Right.

Dave: So, we thought … perhaps … you can sing the first one, and Joanne the second.

Amy: Oh. I see.

Dave: And you can play keyboards when Joanne sings. What do you reckon?

Amy: Oh. Well, it's an idea.

Dave: Great! I'm glad you agree. Isn't it exciting – the contest next week, I mean?

Amy: Oh, yes. But to be honest, I'm a bit nervous. You know, I really want to win and get the chance to make a record but I haven't sung in front of a big crowd for ages.

Dave: Oh, don't worry, Amy – you'll be fine, I know you will.

Amy: Thanks, Dave. Listen – when are we going to London?

Dave: Oh, there's a bus next Saturday at eight thirty. We can spend the afternoon in London, and get ready for the contest in the evening.

Amy: OK. Come on, let's get a move on – the film starts in fifteen minutes.

b Answer the questions.

1 Where are Dave and Amy going after they have coffee?
2 What do Dave and Matt think about Joanne?
3 What does Dave want Amy and Joanne to do in the contest?
4 How does Amy feel about the contest? Why?
5 When and how are Dave and Amy going to London?

8 Everyday English

(a) Find expressions 1–4 from the story. Who says them? Match them with definitions a–d.

1	I <u>see</u>.	a	to say what (I) really think
2	What do you <u>reckon</u>?	b	go quickly
3	<u>to be honest</u>	c	understand
4	<u>get a move on</u>	d	think

(b) Complete the sentences with the <u>underlined</u> words from Exercise 8a.

1 **Fred:** Do you like Marco's new hairstyle?
   Chaz: Well, ... – no, not really, I think it's too short.

2 **Erol:** James hasn't spoken to Jack since last Friday. Do you think they've had an argument?
   Steph: Yes, I .... James is really angry with him.

3 **Annie:** Look – it's eleven o'clock already!
   Daisy: Really? Come on – we need to .... !

4 **Marek:** Sorry I'm late, Miss. I missed the bus.
   Teacher: I .... Well, please don't be late again.

9 Speak and write

(a) Read this email from your American friend, Brad. What kind of information does he want you to give him? Why?

(b) Look at the questions Brad asks. Work with a partner. Ask and answer the questions.

A: *What kinds of things make you laugh?*

B: *Lots of things make me laugh, for example when my little brother makes silly faces, and my dad loses his car keys and gets angry.*

(c) Write your reply to Brad. Write a paragraph to answer each of his questions. You could start like this:

Get Msg   Write Msg   Reply   File   Delete

Hi there!

How are you doing? Haven't heard from you for a long time. Where have you been?

Listen, we're doing a project at school about how different teenagers around the world have fun. I'd really like you to help me, if you can! So, can you tell me:
– what kinds of things make you laugh?
– what things you do to have a good time?
– how often you do them?!
– how long you've done them for?!
– why you think having fun is important.

If you can think of anything else to write, please do! In return, I'll send you some great photos of me and my friends in California.

Thanks very much, and write soon!
Brad

Get Msg   Write Msg   Reply   File   Delete   Stop   Print

Hi Brad
Thanks for your email. Sorry I haven't written sooner, I've ...

Anyway, you want to know how we have fun in ...

For your portfolio

8 A great film!

* Verbs + *-ing* / verbs + infinitive
* Vocabulary: film

1 Read and listen

(a) What is the woman's job? What kinds of things does she have to do? Read the magazine article quickly to find the answers.

(b) 🔊 Read the article again and listen. Answer the questions.

1 Why does Alex love her work?
2 Which job did she <u>not</u> do? Why?
3 Alex's work is dangerous, but she isn't worried. Why not?

(c) Find words in the article with these meanings.

1 A normal job with regular hours: a n_____ -to- _____ job
2 Very frightening: t_____
3 The opposite of *dangerous*: s_____
4 Really hate something: can't s_____ something
5 Get money from a job: e_____ money

(d) Would you like to be a stuntman or stuntwoman? Why / Why not?

It was really terrifying ...

Alex Smithson doesn't have a normal job. She's a stuntwoman in Hollywood movies.

'I did a nine-to-five job for five years, but I hated working in an office so I decided to become a stuntwoman. I much prefer having this job. It's very exciting and I really like doing the stunts,' she says.

What kinds of things does she have to do?
'Well, in action films for example, I often have to jump out of exploding cars or burning buildings. In the thriller *Steel Wings* I had to stand on a plane flying over the mountains. It was really terrifying, but great, too.'

Does she worry about the danger?
She knows she could end up in hospital, but she never thinks about it. 'Of course the work is dangerous. But I don't mind being in dangerous situations and there are lots of people on the film set who check that

everything is safe. I don't want to die in a stunt, and the director doesn't want me to die either.'

What's the most terrifying job she remembers?
'Once they asked me to get into a hole full of snakes. Of course they weren't really dangerous, but I absolutely hate snakes! I refused to go in! I can't stand looking at pictures of snakes, so you can imagine how I felt near real ones!'

Does she ever want to stop?
'No!' Alex says. 'I know that one day I'll be too old, but right now I enjoy doing what I do, I earn a lot of money and I hope to continue for a long time. I can't imagine doing anything else!'

2 Grammar

Verbs + -ing / verbs + infinitive

a Find these words in the text on page 52. Write the verb that <u>follows</u> each one.

1	hated	*working*	7	refused	....
2	decided	....	8	can't stand	....
3	prefer	....	9	enjoy	....
4	like	....	10	hope	....
5	don't mind	....	11	imagine	....
6	don't want	....			

b Write the verbs from Exercise 2a in two lists.

+ -ing	+ infinitive
hate	_decide_

Can you add these verbs to the lists?

agree   learn   love   offer   promise

c (Circle) the correct verbs.

1 I *hate /*(*love*) getting up early. It's the best part of the day!

2 I *don't like / prefer* watching science fiction films on TV. The special effects are better in the cinema.

3 I *prefer / like* watching TV to reading a book.

4 Housework is OK. I *don't mind / hate* tidying my room.

5 I *can't stand / love* writing emails. It's so boring!

d Complete the sentences with the correct form of the verbs.

1 I wasn't feeling well, and I _wanted to leave_ (want/leave) the classroom.

2 You can borrow my bike if you .... (promise/bring) it back at 3 o'clock.

3 When I leave school, I .... (hope/go) to university.

4 My brother's seventeen now, so he's going to .... (learn/drive).

5 My mum was very busy yesterday, so I .... (offer/help) with the cooking.

6 The film was awful, so we .... (decide/leave) before the end.

7 Tom's dad .... (refuse/give) him any money to buy some new trainers.

e Complete the sentences. Use the correct form of the verbs in the box.

get up   eat   be   watch   dance   go
do   ~~listen~~   help   let   cook

1 My sister hates _listening_ to CDs – but she really enjoys .... DVDs.

2 My parents don't like .... out in restaurants. They prefer .... at home.

3 I don't mind .... early in summer, when it's light in the mornings.

4 Jane really wanted .... to the party and her parents finally agreed .... her go.

5 My dad can't stand .... the ironing, so I often offer .... him.

6 I love .... and I hope .... a dancer when I leave school!

3 Speak

a Work with a partner. Say which of these things you don't mind / like / enjoy / love / hate / can't stand doing, and why.

write emails   talk on the phone   walk
cycle   go to parties   go to the cinema
read books   read magazines   give presents
get presents

A: *I can't stand cycling!*

B: *Really? I like cycling, but only when it's sunny! And I really enjoy going to parties.*

b Work with partner. Say which of the things in Exercise 3a you prefer doing and why.

A: *I prefer writing emails to talking on the phone. It's quicker!*

B: *Me too. I prefer reading books to reading magazines ...*

Look

I prefer writing emails **to** talking on the phone. (= I think writing emails is better.)

c Now think back to last week or last month. Tell your partner something you:

- promised to do
- offered to do
- decided to do
- refused to do
- agreed to do
- wanted to do (but didn't!)

A: *I promised to tidy my bedroom, but I didn't!*

B: *I refused to give my brother some money.*

4 Vocabulary
Films

thriller

a 🔊 Listen to the music from different types of films and match them with the pictures. Write 1–8 in the boxes.

b 🔊 Write the type of film under each picture. Use the words in the box. Then listen, check and repeat.

> ~~thriller~~ western comedy romance action horror
> science fiction drama

c Can you think of an example for each type of film in Exercise 4b?

d Match words 1–7 with definitions a–g.

1 special effects   a the music in a film
2 director   b someone who is in a film
3 storyline   c the words the people in the film learn
4 actor/actress   d a place where they film parts of a film
5 script   e amazing images often produced with computers
6 soundtrack   f what happens in the film
7 film set   g the person who gives instructions to the actors and cameramen

e Complete the sentences with words 1–7 in Exercise 4d.

1 My favourite _actress_ is Christina Ricci. I think she's great!
2 The film I watched last night had a really exciting _____ . The ending was a complete surprise!
3 If you want to act in a film, you have to read the _____ first.
4 The _____ of *Jurassic Park* was Steven Spielberg.
5 I've got the _____ of the film *Paris Texas* on CD. It's great music.
6 Science fiction films often have great _____ _____ .
7 Last year, they made a film in my old school, and it became a _____ _____ with lots of cameras and actors everywhere.

5 Speak

Work with a partner or small group. Ask and answer the questions.

- How often do you go to the cinema?
- When was the last time you watched a film? What did you see?
- What is your favourite film? Why? Who is your favourite actor/actress?
- What types of films do you like? Why?
- Do you prefer going to the cinema or watching videos? Why?
- Have you ever met a famous actor or actress?

6 Pronunciation

Consonant clusters

🔊 Turn to page 120.

7 Read

Look at the photos and read about the people. Then read the film reviews. Which film(s) do you recommend for each person? Why? (Be careful, there are more films than people!)

Carolina (17) loves romances, beautiful scenery and stories with happy endings. She hates science fiction and horror films.

Kasia (24) wants to see an action movie with her friends.

Serkan (17) loves watching all types of films but today he'd like to see a comedy.

Sandra (9) is going to be ten next week and her parents want to take her to the cinema for her birthday.

Hugo (21) likes science fiction films but can't stand watching gun fights.

Rangers

Set in Mexico in the year 3000. This film has an exciting storyline and even better special effects.

Film of the month – don't miss it!

Yesterday

Wonderful film set in Venice, by the famous director John Woodall. A young couple are in love and want to get married. The problem is, their parents aren't happy …

Great soundtrack and beautiful photography.

High School Days

Three teenage boys meet at Stafford High School. They decide to start a band together and that's when the fun really starts …

Funny, with a clever script.

Oregon Adventure

Set in the early 19th century, this is a story about a long journey west across the States and the problems the pioneers had on the way. Both funny and sad with a great soundtrack.

If you like westerns, this is the film for you.

Freddy

A boy discovers he has magic powers, but what happens when he visits his grandparents?

Fun for all the family.

Busters

Actor and singer John Maskell stars in this movie set in Los Angeles. Lots of guns and lots of car chases. If you want excitement, watch this!

Don't watch it if you hate the sight of blood!

 **Don't miss it!**   ●●●●○ **Very good**
●●●○○ **Good**   ●●○○○ **OK**   ●○○○○ **Stay at home!**

8 Listen

(a) 🔊 Listen to James and Karen talking about one of the films in the Exercise 7. Which film are they talking about?

(b) 🔊 Listen again and complete the sentences with the words in the box.

It's about	acting	ending
It stars	It's set in	

1 _____ the future.
2 _____ Peter Arnold.
3 _____ a man who wants to change the world.
4 I didn't like the _____ at all and I thought the _____ was stupid.

9 Speak

Work with a partner. Tell each other about a film you've seen. Use the ideas and language from Exercise 8.

I saw … last week …

It's about … and it's set in …

I really liked … but I thought the … was …

Culture in mind

10 Read

(a) Can you name the people in the photos? What do you know about each of them?

Many people dream of being a film star. Successful Hollywood stars often earn millions of dollars, and they can buy almost anything they want. They live in fantastic houses in places like Beverley Hills, and they wear expensive designer clothes. They drive the best cars in the world and their work often takes them to wonderful places. They can have amazing holidays, and can stay in luxury hotels or sail in private yachts. They go to Hollywood parties, and can enjoy seeing their photographs on the cover of magazines, and their faces on the big screen. To us it seems that they have everything. But are they really happy?

I don't think the lives of Hollywood film stars are as easy as we think. For many of them, life is like living in a goldfish bowl, and everyone can see everything they do. They are followed by the paparazzi wherever they go and we can read all about their private lives in newspapers and magazines. All this means that many film stars have found it difficult to lead a normal life. Macaulay Culkin became famous after the film *Home Alone* when he was only ten years old. He didn't always have an easy life at home and stopped acting for a time. Marilyn Monroe – a big Hollywood star in the 1950s – died in 1962, only 36 and very unhappy. The young 1980s star River Phoenix died when he was only 23.

Not all film stars die young, of course, but they often have other problems. They have to look young and beautiful, and some of them spend thousands of dollars on cosmetic surgery. Many Hollywood marriages don't last very long. Richard Gere and Cindy Crawford, Tom Cruise and Nicole Kidman, Kate Winslet and Jim Threapleton: these are just some of the film star marriages that have failed.

(b) Amy wrote an article for her school web magazine. Read her article quickly and choose the best title.

1   Why I wouldn't like to be a film star
2   Are stars' lives as perfect as we think?
3   How to be a successful film star

(c) Answer the questions.

1   What does Amy's article say are the good things about being a film star?
2   Amy mentions three main difficulties that famous stars can have – what are they?

(d) What is the meaning of the underlined words from Amy's article?

1   designer clothes (paragraph 1)
2   luxury hotels (paragraph 1)
3   a goldfish bowl (paragraph 2)
4   the paparazzi (paragraph 2)
5   cosmetic surgery (paragraph 3)

It's not true that all stars have problems, and I'm sure many really do have great lives. But unless we become stars ourselves in future, we'll never really know what it's like to be famous, will we?

11 Listen

Amy and Mike are talking about Amy's article on Macaulay Culkin. Listen and complete this information about him.

Macaulay Culkin was born on 26 August, 1980 in ¹_____ . He started his career in the theatre when he was ²_____ years old. He made his first film in ³_____ . He won an award as Best Young Actor in ⁴_____ for his part in *Home Alone*. After *Home Alone*, he became the ⁵_____ -paid child actor of all time.

Macaulay stopped acting when he was ⁶_____ , and only started again when he was ⁷_____ . In 1998, he married an actress called Rachel Miner – both Macaulay and Rachel were only ⁸_____ years old – but they separated in ⁹_____ .

Discussion box

Work in pairs or small groups. Discuss these questions together.

1 Is it great to be a Hollywood film star? Are there more advantages or disadvantages?

2 Can you think of any other film stars who have had problems? Tell your partner(s) about them.

3 Do you enjoy reading about stars' lives in newspapers or magazines? Why / Why not?

4 Do famous stars in your country have as many problems as famous Hollywood stars? Why / Why not, do you think?

12 Write

a Read Dave's film review for his school magazine. Match the headings with the paragraphs. Write A, B and C in the boxes.

1 Dave's opinion of the film ☐
2 Facts about the film ☐
3 The storyline ☐

b Write a short review of a film for your school magazine. Use the language from page 55 and Dave's review to help you.

A Last week I went to see *Days of Sun*. It's about a 21-year-old English girl, Julia Ford, who goes to Canada for the summer. There she meets a Canadian boy, Mike Finch. They become very good friends and fall in love. They want to marry, but Julia doesn't want to leave her family in England, and Mike can't leave Canada because his mother is ill and he promises to look after her at home.

B The film is set in Vancouver and London. The director is James Harley, and it stars Alice Ray as Julia and Frank Bussell as Mike.

C I think *Days of Sun* is a fantastic film. The soundtrack is excellent, and the storyline is exciting. I really liked the film because it's happy and sad at the same time. I don't usually like watching romantic films, but I'm very glad I decided to watch this, and I might watch it again in future!

Module 2 Check your progress

1 Grammar

a Complete the questions with the correct question tags.

1 You like this music, _don't you_?
2 Your sister goes to my school, _____?
3 His father's French, _____?
4 We're late, _____?
5 They aren't at home, _____?
6 She hasn't been to San Francisco, _____?
7 He can't cook, _____?
8 You won't forget the CDs, _____?
9 They didn't like the film, _____?
10 You went shopping yesterday, _____?   **9**

b Complete the sentences. Use the present simple passive form of the verbs.

1 Chocolate _is made_ (make) from cocoa beans.
2 Many films _____ (produce) in Hollywood.
3 The Olympics _____ (hold) every four years.
4 This book _____ (not write) in English.
5 Thousands of Beatles CDs _____ (sell) every year.
6 How many cans of Coke _____ (buy) every day?
7 How often _____ the World Cup _____ (hold)?   **6**

c Complete the sentences with the correct form of the present perfect simple.

1 John's _just had_ (just have) his breakfast.
2 A: Would you like some chocolate?
   B: No, thanks. I _____ (already have) some.
3 _____ you _____ (buy) your sister a present yet?
4 We _____ (already finish) our homework.
5 _____ Marta _____ (see) the film yet?
6 My parents _____ (just come) home. I'll phone you later.
7 They're late, they _____ (not arrive) yet.   **6**

d Complete the sentences. Use the correct form of *let* or *be allowed to*.

1 We _let_ (+) our dog go into the living room, but _she isn't allowed to_ (−) go into the bedrooms.
2 We _____ (−) eat in class.
3 My parents _____ (−) me play football in the garden.
4 You _____ (+) take photographs here.
5 My brother _____ (+) me use his camera.
6 In Britain, when you're 17 you _____ (+) drive a car.   **5**

e Complete the sentences. Use the correct form of the present perfect simple and *for* or *since*.

1 I _haven't eaten_ (not eat) any fast food _since_ last month.
2 My dad _____ (be) ill in bed _____ four days.
3 My cousins _____ (live) in their house _____ 20 years.
4 I _____ (not see) Jane _____ 10 o'clock.
5 I really like this CD, but I _____ (not listen) to it _____ a long time.
6 My sister's boyfriend _____ (phone) her eight times _____ Friday!
7 We _____ (not eat) anything _____ breakfast.   **6**

f Circle the correct words.

1 I don't mind (doing)/ to do the washing up, but I prefer (cooking)/ to cook.
2 I'll lend you my CDs, if you promise giving / to give them back tomorrow.
3 We really enjoy listening / to listen to music.
4 I've decided studying / to study hard, because I hope going / to go to university.
5 I can't stand putting / to put the rubbish out – I always refuse doing / to do it!
6 My sister offered helping / to help my dad.   **7**

2 Vocabulary

(a) Put the letters in order to find British or North American English words. Then write them in the table.

> avmentep   ~~mentatrap~~   roustres   yawbus
> flit   geagrab

British English	North American English
flat	1 _apartment_
2	elevator
3	pants
rubbish	4 ....
5	sidewalk
underground	6 ....

☐ 5

(b) Read clues 1–7 and fill in the puzzle with words to describe a person's age. What's the mystery word?

Crossword with letters: 1 ...L..., 2 ...N, 3 ...I..., 4 ...I..., 5 ...D..., 6 ...S..., 7 ...A...

1 In Britain, if you're over 18, you're an ....

2 The opposite of *old*.

3 Someone who is six or seven years old.

4 Someone who is about 50 is .... – aged.

5 A more polite word for *old*.

6 This person is over 65 years old and doesn't work any more.

7 If you're 14, you're a ....

☐ 7

(c) Write the words in the lists.

> director   script   actress   storyline   thriller
> science fiction   western   soundtrack   ~~horror~~

People	Kinds of films	Other words about film
actor	_horror_	special effects
....	....	....
....	....	....
	....	

☐ 8

3 Everyday English

Complete the dialogue with the words in the box.

> get a move on   I see   nice one
> I reckon   ~~sure~~   to be honest

Mel: Jim! Do you know what time it is?

Jim: 1 _Sure_ – it's 7.30.

Mel: That's right. 2 .... , or we'll be late for the cinema!

Jim: Well, Mel, 3 .... , I don't think I want to go.

Mel: Oh, 4 .... Why not?

Jim: Well, it's another *Star Wars* film and 5 .... it won't be very good.

Mel: OK. Oh, I forgot to tell you. I asked Anna to come with us.

Jim: You asked Anna? 6 .... , Mel! OK, I'll come with you.

Mel: Good. Put your coat on, and let's go!

☐ 5

How did you do?

Tick (✓) a box for each section.

Total score	😊 Very good	😐 OK	😞 Not very good
☐ 64			
Grammar	30 – 39	24 – 29	less than 24
Vocabulary	16 – 20	11 – 15	less than 11
Everyday English	4 – 5	3	less than 3

Module 3
Weird and wonderful

YOU WILL LEARN ABOUT ...

- Some natural disasters ....
- Why tsunami waves happen ....
- A tribe in Borneo ....
- Life in Australia ....
- Intelligence and memory ....
- A brilliant young musician ....
- The history of popular music ....

   ✱ Can you match each photo with a topic?

YOU WILL LEARN HOW TO ...

Speak
- Talk about events in history
- Describe an imaginary dream
- Talk about your home
- Discuss stereotypes
- Talk about how you learn
- Exchange information about a pop singer
- Talk about music
- Discuss fashion and the history of pop music

Write
- A newspaper article about a disaster
- An email about your holiday plans
- An entry for a competition
- A letter about your favourite type of music

Read
- An article about tsunamis
- A holiday brochure and email about a trip to Borneo
- An article about life in Australia
- An article about your memory
- An article about a brilliant young musician
- A web page about the history of pop music

Listen
- A radio interview about an earthquake
- Descriptions of different types of homes
- An interview about different types of intelligence
- People talking about music and instruments

Use grammar

Can you match the names of the grammar points with the examples?

Past simple passive	I've **been working** all morning.
Definite and indefinite articles	You **don't have to** listen, but you **mustn't** make any noise.
too much / too many / not enough	The city **was destroyed** by the earthquake.
will vs. *going to*	**Someone** did it, but **no one** knows who it was.
Determiners (*everyone/no one* etc.)	There's **a** basin in **the** bedroom.
mustn't vs. *don't have to*	**We're going to visit** the USA this summer.
Present perfect continuous	There were **too many** people and **not enough** chairs.

Use vocabulary

Can you think of two more examples for each topic?

Disasters	Homes	Remembering/ forgetting	Music
avalanche	flat	remember	jazz
volcano	cottage	memory	guitar
....	....	....	....
....	....	....	....

9 Disaster!

* Past simple passive
* *a, an* or *the*
* Vocabulary: disasters

1 Vocabulary and listening

a

b

c

d

e

a 🔊 Match the words with the photos. Write 1–6 in the boxes. Then listen, check and repeat.

> 1 an earthquake   2 an avalanche   3 a tsunami   4 a nuclear bomb   5 a volcano

b The event in photo d is different from the other disasters. Why?

c 🔊 Look at the photo. Where and when do you think the earthquake happened? Listen to the first part of an interview about the earthquake and check your ideas.

d Check that you understand the words in the box. Then use the words to complete the summary of the story in Exercise 1c.

> killed ~~happened~~ destroyed lost
> buildings injured 3,000 money

> The earthquake *happened* early in the morning. Over _____ people were _____ and about 225,000 were _____ . Almost 500 _____ were _____ and a lot of _____ was _____ – a total of about $400,000,000.

e 🔊 Listen to the second part of the interview and check your answers.

2 Grammar

Past simple passive

a Look at the example. <u>Underline</u> other examples of the past simple passive in the summary in Exercise 1d. Then complete the rule.

*Over 3,000 people **were killed**.*

> **Rule:** to form the past simple passive, use the past simple form of the verb _____ and the _____ _____ .

b Complete the sentences. Use the past simple passive form of the verbs.

1 This photo _____ (take) two years ago.   *was taken*
2 She's really upset because her bicycle _____ (steal) last night.
3 These houses _____ (build) in the 17th century.
4 This book _____ (write) in 2001.
5 Computers _____ (not use) in our school until 1985.

c Rewrite the sentences. Use the past simple passive.

1 Someone found the dead man late last night.
   The dead man was found late last night.
2 They robbed the house at midnight.
   The house _____ .
3 They made a film about the San Francisco earthquake.
   A film _____ .
4 They completed the Empire State Building in 1932.
   _____ .
5 Someone broke the classroom window last night.
   _____ .

3 Pronunciation

'Silent' letters

🔊 Turn to page 121.

4 Speak

a Work with a partner. Student A: look at your questions on this page. Student B: turn to page 122 and look at your questions. Ask and answer the questions. Use the past simple passive. Student A: you start.

b When you've finished your teacher will give you the answers. Compare your results with other pairs.

> **Student A**
>
> 1 When / the Berlin wall / knock down? In 1989 or 1979?
>   *When was the Berlin wall knocked down?*
> 2 Who / *The Lord of the Rings* / write by? J.R.R. Tolkien or William Golding?
> 3 Which group / the song *Help!* / sing by? The Rolling Stones or The Beatles?
> 4 Where / the Statue of Liberty / build? In Paris or in New York?
> 5 When / American President John F. Kennedy / kill? In 1949 or in 1963?

5 Read

a Read the text quickly to find the answers to these questions.

1 Where does the name 'tsunami' come from?

2 How high can tsunamis be?

3 What causes a tsunami?

T S U N A M I

the giant wave

A Natural disasters such as volcanic eruptions, fires, floods and avalanches happen every year, somewhere in the world. But there is another, and perhaps even more dangerous, natural disaster, which we do not hear about very often. A tsunami is a huge wave that can cause terrible damage and destruction.

B Tsunami is a Japanese word that means 'harbour wave'. But why do tsunamis happen? Tsunamis are usually caused by earthquakes at the bottom of the sea. At first, the wave in the sea is quite small, but it moves very quickly. When the wave gets close to the coast, the ocean floor makes it grow enormously. By the time it reaches the coast it has become huge. Some tsunamis can be 30 metres high.

C These giant waves can hit Japan, Indonesia, Central America and South America. In 1960, there was a big tsunami in the Pacific Ocean. Tsunamis do not happen very often, but Hawaii now has a 'tsunami-watch' station that watches for the next one to come. The station was opened to warn people and give them time to protect themselves against the killer waves.

D On December 26th, 2004, there was an earthquake at the bottom of the Indian Ocean that measured 8.5 on the Richter Scale. The earthquake started a giant wave that hit the coast of Indonesia, Thailand, Sri Lanka, the Maldives, India, Bangladesh and Burma. The wave travelled at around 800 kilometres per hour over the 4,500 kilometre-wide Indian Ocean. It hit the east coast of Africa seven hours after the earthquake. Over 300,000 people were killed. Whole towns were destroyed, and thousands of people lost their homes. Other countries offered $7 billion to help. It was the world's biggest earthquake for forty years. There was no warning station in the Indian Ocean.

b Match the topics 1–4 with paragraphs A–D in the text. Write A–D in the boxes.

1 The causes of a tsunami ☐

2 A disaster caused by a tsunami ☐

3 What is a tsunami? ☐

4 What have the Hawaiians done? ☐

c Read the text again and put the pictures in the correct order. Write 1–4 in the boxes.

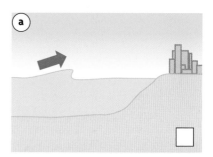

a ☐

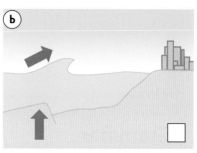

b ☐

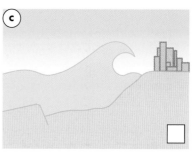

c ☐

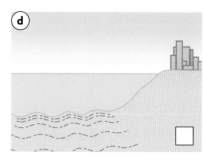

d ☐

d Find words in the text with these meanings.

1 Extremely big (paragraph A)

----

2 The place where the sea meets the land (paragraph B)

----

3 The bottom of the sea (2 words, paragraph B)

----

4 Make safe (paragraph C)

----

6 Grammar

a/an or *the*

a Read the text. <u>Underline</u> *a*, *an*, *the* and the nouns they are with.

Two famous disasters that have happened were <u>an</u> <u>earthquake</u> and a volcanic eruption.

The earthquake happened in 1964 in Alaska and was the strongest earthquake that was ever recorded. The volcano erupted about 2,000 years ago. It destroyed a Roman town called Pompeii.

b Complete the rule.

> **Rule:**
>
> • Use _____ or _____ + noun to talk about something for the first time.
>
>   *I had **a banana** and **an apple** for breakfast.*
>
> • Use _____ + noun when it is clear which thing or person you are talking about.
>
>   ***The banana** was very good, but **the apple** was horrible.*

c Complete the sentences with *a*, *an* or *the*.

1 I've got two bicycles, _____ green one and _____ grey one. I got _____ green bike as a birthday present when was 12. I bought _____ grey bike with my own money.

2 I read _____ newspaper story about _____ new plane yesterday. _____ plane can carry 3,000 people, but _____ story didn't say when they will finish making it.

3 My father drives _____ old car. He loves it! It was made in 1960, and it looks really beautiful. Last week he had _____ phone call from _____ woman in London. My father didn't know _____ woman, but she offered him £10,000 for _____ car!

7 Speak

a Two students are describing an imaginary dream. Complete the dialogue with *a/an* or *the*.

A: Last night I dreamed that I was somewhere in ¹_____ wood.

B: In ²_____ wood there were lots of strange things. First I saw ³_____ house.

A: ⁴_____ house was made of chocolate. When I walked closer, ⁵_____ woman opened the door.

B: ⁶_____ woman was very old and she was wearing big glasses. She said, 'You can eat some of ⁷_____ chocolate, but you have to give me ⁸_____ present.'

A: I didn't know what to give her. But then I remembered. I had ⁹_____ photo of my dog in my pocket.

B: I gave it to ¹⁰_____ woman and she looked at it. Suddenly I saw ¹¹_____ giant cat.

A: ¹²_____ cat was bigger than ¹³_____ elephant. I was scared, but then I had ¹⁴_____ idea ...

b Work with a partner. Invent another dream. Use the dialogue in Exercise 7a to help you. The student who says the last sentence is the winner.

Let's talk about it later

8 Read and listen

(a) 🔊 Where are the people in the story?
How does Amy feel? Why, do you think?
Read, listen and check your answers.

Joanne: What's up with her?

Dave: Who, Amy? Nothing – I think she's just nervous, and she likes to be alone sometimes.

Joanne: Oh, I see. Well, look, you two, there's something I want to talk to you about.

Matt: Oh yeah? What's that, Joanne?

Joanne: Well, remember the first rehearsal? Just the three of us? We haven't been as good as that since Amy joined us.

Matt: What are you trying to say, Joanne?

Joanne: Well, I think perhaps after the contest, we should get our own band together, a three person band, without Amy. What do you reckon?

Matt: Well, I don't know. The band was started by Amy and Dave. It doesn't seem right, does it?

Dave: I know what you mean, Matt. But Joanne's got a point too.

Joanne: So, do you agree then, Dave?

Dave: Well, let me think about it, Joanne, OK? Let's talk about it later.

Amy: So what were you all talking about just now?

Dave: Well, to be honest, Joanne was asking Matt and me if we wanted to make a new band after the contest – the three of us.

Amy: What!? I hope you said no, Dave.

Dave: Yeah, sort of.

Amy: Sort of? What does that mean, Dave? Do you want to get rid of me, or what?

Dave: No, Amy. Of course not. I just said perhaps we should talk about it later, that's all.

Amy: Dave! How could you?!

(b) Match the two parts of the sentences.

1	Amy is	a	to think about Joanne's idea.
2	Joanne wants	b	nervous about the contest.
3	Matt thinks	c	that Dave wants her to leave the band.
4	Dave wants	d	about Joanne's idea.
5	Amy asks Dave	e	to start a new band without Amy.
6	Dave tells Amy	f	that Joanne's idea isn't right.
7	Amy thinks	g	what he was talking to Matt and Joanne about.

9 Everyday English

a Find expressions 1–4 in the story. Who says them? How do you say these things in your language?

1 What's up with her?
2 get rid of me
3 Joanne's got a point
4 sort of

b Complete the sentences with the underlined words from Exercise 9a.

1 **Steve:** Hey Andy. You look sad! .... you?

 Andy: Oh, Anna doesn't want to see me any more.

2 **Marta:** Ella said the band was too loud and I think she's .... My ears hurt!

 Luisa: Yes, mine do too!

3 **Chris:** Have you done all your homework, Ben?

 Ben: Well, ... I've done some, but I couldn't do the difficult questions.

4 **Miguel:** We must .... those old books. We never read them!

 Enrique: OK. But please don't throw them away without asking me first.

10 Write

a Read the newspaper story about a disaster in Dover. What happened? How did it happen?

MAN RESCUED FROM SEA

A 28-year-old man was rescued by helicopter yesterday in Dover after he fell into the sea near his holiday home.

The accident happened while the man, John Carter, was walking along a cliff. He was blown off by a very strong wind and fell into the sea, 30 metres below. Luckily, a woman saw Mr Carter in the water soon afterwards and she called the police rescue service. He was taken to hospital with a broken arm.

Last night Mr Carter said from his hospital bed, 'I'm very lucky to be alive. My life was saved by the woman who called the police. I can't thank her enough.'

b Look at the pictures of a forest fire. Describe what you can see in each picture. Use some of the words in the box.

catch fire	strong winds	very hot weather
leave their homes	burn	drop a cigarette
dry leaves	not control the fire	

c Write a newspaper story about the forest fire. Use the story in Exercise 10a and the phrases in Exercise 10b to help you.

Paragraph 1:   What happened, where and when?
Paragraph 2:   How did it happen?
Paragraph 3:   What was the result?

For your portfolio

10 A place to stay

* *too many / much + not enough*
* *will* vs. *be going to*
* Vocabulary: homes

1 Read and listen

a Look at the pictures from the holiday brochure. What kind of holiday is it? Where is it? Read the brochure quickly to check your ideas.

Want an adventure? Spend ten days in BORNEO

GETTING THERE

Fly from London to Jakarta, and then to Kuching in Borneo. After two days in Kuching, we take you on a trip you'll never forget – up the river in a longboat to visit an Iban village.

WHAT YOU'LL DO

Friendly Iban people in traditional clothes will show you the village and introduce you to their lifestyle. They'll invite you to join their traditional dances, and to visit the farms where they work. You'll also go on a trek into the jungle, to see orang-utans and crocodiles.

WHAT YOU'LL SEE

You'll see the amazing Iban longhouses. A longhouse is like a street of separate apartments, all under one roof. Sometimes 30 families live together, perhaps 150 or more people in one big house. The longhouses are built on wooden poles about three metres high – this keeps out water when there are floods (and wild animals, too!). Most visitors stay in the longhouses.

b Read the brochure again and find out:

1 the name of the tribe visitors meet on this holiday
2 where this tribe lives
3 what visitors do there

c 🔊 Annie Miller went on this holiday and wrote an email to a friend about it. Read and listen to her email. What was she happy about? What problems did she have?

Get Msg   Write Msg   Reply   File   Delete   Stop   Print

Hi John!
Well, I'm back! I had a great time in Borneo – really fascinating.

Kuching was interesting, but I don't think we spent enough time there. When we left to go on the river, there were too many people for the longboat, so we travelled to the village in a bus. The village was fascinating. I loved the longhouses, but there weren't enough rooms for all of us to sleep there, so we had to sleep in tents. The first night was great, but I ate too much delicious Iban food, and so I felt ill the next morning! The second night wasn't as good because there wasn't enough food for everyone. After that there was a jungle trek – lots of interesting things there, but not enough time to see everything.

Anyway, I'll see you next weekend and show you all my photos.

See you then!

Annie

2 Grammar

too much / many + not enough

a Look at the examples.

*I ate **too much food**.*
*... but **not enough time** to see everything!*

b Underline other examples of *too much / too many* and *not enough* in Annie's email on page 68.

c Look at examples 1–4. What's the difference in meaning between *too much / many* and *a lot (of)*?

There are a lot of tourists.

There are too many tourists.

There's a lot of traffic.

There's too much traffic.

d Look at sentences 2 and 4 in Exercise 2c. Complete the rule.

> **Rule:** Use *too* _____ with countable nouns, and *too* _____ with _____ nouns.

e Complete the sentences with *too much* or *too many*.

I always get _____ homework!

There are _____ people in here!

I think I've eaten _____ food.

The problem is, I've got _____ CDs.

f Look at the examples. Then complete the rule.

*There **weren't enough** rooms.*
*There **wasn't enough** food.*

> **Rule:** Use *(not) enough* with both _____ and _____ nouns.

g Complete the text with *too much*, *too many* or *(not) enough*.

I don't really like my town. Every summer, <u>too many</u> tourists come here, so there are ¹_____ cars in the streets, and that means there's ²_____ noise. There aren't ³_____ places for teenagers to go, either. There are lots of shops but there are always ⁴_____ people in them! And most of the clothes shops are for old people — there ⁵_____ shops for young people like me!

h Work with a partner. Make true sentences about you.

> clothes   money   CDs   homework
> television   time

A: *I haven't got enough money.*
B: *Yes, same here! And I always get too much homework.*

3 Pronunciation

Sound and spelling: *-ough*

🔊 Turn to page 121.

4 Vocabulary

Homes

(a) 🔊 Match the words in the box with the pictures.
Write the words in the spaces. Then listen, check and repeat.

> a detached house   a block of flats   a housing estate   a cottage
> a bungalow   a semi-detached house   a caravan   terraced houses

(b) In which pictures can you see these things?

> a chimney   a garden   a garage   a TV aerial   a gate

a

b

c

d

e

f

g

h

(c) Look at the pictures and answer the questions.

1   Where can you probably find *stairs*?

2   Where do you think you can find a *lift*?

3   Where do the families live on one *floor*?

5 Listen

🔊 Listen to six people talking about where they live. Which picture shows each speaker's home? Write 1–6 in the boxes.

6 Speak

Work with a partner. Talk about where you live.

I live in a block of flats. Our flat is on the first floor. We've got two bedrooms.

7 Grammar

will vs. *be going to*

a 🔊 Jake is planning a trip to China. Read and listen to his conversation with his grandmother. What is he going to do in there?

Gran: So Jake, I hear you're going to China next month!

Jake: Yes. I'm going to visit a place called Qinghai. There are lots of Tibetan people there and I'm going to stay with them in one of their tents.

Gran: How exciting! Have you packed everything yet?

Jake: No, I'm not going until next month!

Gran: Well, you mustn't forget to pack warm clothes. I'm sure it's very cold there at night!

Jake: I'll pack some jumpers.

Gran: And don't forget some comfortable walking boots.

Jake: But I haven't got any good boots.

Gran: Don't worry, I'll give you some money to buy some.

Jake: Oh thanks a lot, Gran!

Gran: So, how long are you going for?

Jake: For three weeks altogether. I can't wait!

Gran: Well, I'd like to hear from you when you're there.

Jake: Of course, Gran. I won't forget to send you a postcard when I arrive.

Look

We don't usually say ... *going ~~to go~~* ...
- I'm going to ~~go to~~ school tomorrow.
- She's going to ~~go to~~ America next year.

b Look at the examples. <u>Underline</u> other examples of *will* and *going to* in the dialogue in Exercise 7a. Then complete the rule.

I'm going to visit a place called Qinghai.
I won't forget to send you a postcard.

> **Rule:**
> - For decisions and plans made before the moment of speaking, use _____ .
> - For decisions made at the moment of speaking, and for offers and promises, use _____ / _____ .

c Circle the correct words in the sentences.

1 A: I can't carry all these books, they're much too heavy!
   B: Give them to me, (*I'll carry them*) / *I'm going to carry them* for you.

2 Tom's really excited because *he's going* / *he'll go* on holiday tomorrow.

3 A: I'm really hot in here!
   B: Really? OK, *I'll open* / *I'm going to open* the window.

4 A: Have you got any plans for Friday night?
   B: Yes, *we'll see* / *we're going to see* a film.

5 My sister's really nervous because *she's going to take* / *she'll take* her driving test tomorrow.

6 A: I haven't got enough money to go out.
   B: Don't worry, *I'll lend* / *I'm going to lend* you some.

7 A: What would you like to drink?
   B: *I'll have* / *I'm going to have* an orange juice, please.

Culture in mind

8 Read

(a) Look at the title and pictures. 'Down under' means 'in Australia'. What do you know about Australia?

(b) What do you think are the main differences between life in Australia and life in Britain? Read the text quickly to check your ideas.

(c) Answer the questions.

1 What do a lot of British people think about Australians?
2 What do Australians often do at weekends?
3 What do Megan's British cousins like / not like about Australia?
4 What does Josh say about teenagers in Britain and Australia?
5 What does Josh say about Australian people?

Discussion box

Work in small groups or pairs. Discuss these questions together.

1 Matthew says that the idea many people have about Australian people is 'a stereotype'. What does this mean?

2 Are there any stereotypes about people in your country? If so, what are they?

3 Many people think stereotypes are dangerous. Why, do you think?

LIFE 'DOWN UNDER'

In the 1980s, the *Crocodile Dundee* films were big hits. Starring Australian actor and comedian Paul Hogan, the films showed us what Australian people are like: relaxed, good-humoured, suntanned, and ready to fight crocodiles. But is that really what Australians are like?

Matthew Taylor moved to Australia from the UK in 1973, when he was 18 years old. Now living in Adelaide, and married with two teenage children, Matthew and his family go back to Britain every two years, and they are in a good position to see the differences between the way of life in the two countries.

'People in Britain think that Australians all live by the beach, and swim and surf all day!' says Matthew.

'Of course that's a stereotype. But it's partly true!'

Matthew's 15-year-old daughter Megan agrees. 'Here in Australia people live a more "outdoor" life, because the weather's generally good,' says Megan. 'For example, we have barbecues almost every weekend – and we're lucky because we've got a swimming pool at our house. My cousins from the UK love it when they come and visit us! They love the pool, and the fact that

Australian houses are often bigger. There are lots of different types of houses, of course, but more families here live in a big house with rooms all on one floor. In Britain, a typical house for the average family has two floors and three bedrooms. The only thing they don't like is the insects – we have lots here, including mosquitoes, so we have screens on the doors and windows.'

Her brother Josh (18) doesn't see so many differences. 'I think family

9 Write

a Read about holidays A and B and answer questions 1–3.

1 How long is each holiday?

2 The two holidays have two things in common – what are they?

3 What do you learn on each type of holiday?

A

Want a holiday with a difference?

Come to Leasdale Farm and spend four days living with a family and working on a real English farm! You stay in rooms in a converted barn, and all meals are provided.

Our guests help to look after the animals and they learn how a farm really works!

Healthy and fun – Leasdale Farm holidays are great for teenagers and all the family!

B

Learn English with a family in Britain!

Spend ten days living in a British city with a friendly family. You'll have your own room in the family's house, and you'll find out what life in Britain is really like.

Your family will give you all your meals, and they'll take you to interesting places. You'll get the chance to meet lots of their friends – and of course your English will get much better!

Homestay English is a great way to learn!

life is basically the same in Britain and Australia,' he says. 'I think we do the same things as kids in the UK. Music, sport, cinema, dancing – it's not so different. But Megan's right that we can do more outside. Also, things are quite relaxed here. The clothes people wear, for example, and the way they talk to each other. I think Australians are really friendly. I mean, British people are friendly too, of course, but anyone who visits Australia gets a warm welcome. It's great here – I think the Australian way of life is the best in the world!'

The whole family agrees – and none of them have ever fought a crocodile!

b Nadia is going on holiday A. Read her email to her friend. Who is going with her on holiday? What does she promise to do after her holiday?

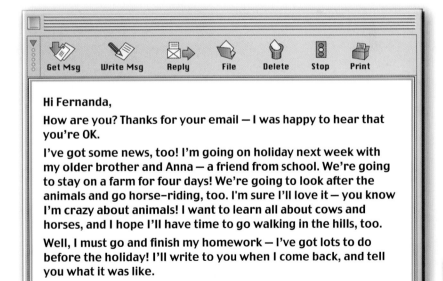

Hi Fernanda,

How are you? Thanks for your email — I was happy to hear that you're OK.

I've got some news, too! I'm going on holiday next week with my older brother and Anna — a friend from school. We're going to stay on a farm for four days! We're going to look after the animals and go horse-riding, too. I'm sure I'll love it — you know I'm crazy about animals! I want to learn all about cows and horses, and I hope I'll have time to go walking in the hills, too.

Well, I must go and finish my homework — I've got lots to do before the holiday! I'll write to you when I come back, and tell you what it was like.

Take care

Love

Nadia

c Imagine you are going on holiday B. Write an email to an English-speaking friend and tell him/her what you're going to do. Use the information and Nadia's email to help you.

For your portfolio

11 Your mind

* Determiners (*everyone / no one etc.*)
* *must / mustn't* vs. *don't have to*
* Vocabulary: remembering and forgetting

1 Read and listen

a 🔊 Before you read, try a fun memory test. Listen to your teacher's instructions.

b Look at the title of the text. How do you think you can improve your memory? Read the text quickly to check your ideas.

How to improve your memory

The human brain is very powerful. The average adult human brain only weighs about 1.4 kilograms, but it can hold much more information than most computers. However, there is another difference between humans and computers. Computers don't forget information they are given, but humans often do. No one remembers everything, and luckily we don't usually have to. But some people have a better memory than other people – or at least, some people can remember some things better than other people can. For example, Mozart once listened to a piece of music for the first time, and then he immediately sat down at the piano and played it perfectly from memory. But his memory wasn't good in other ways – his wife often had to remind him what day it was!

Everyone can improve their memory if they want to. Here are some tips. All of them are helpful, but none of them can make your memory 100% perfect.

* Try to use new information immediately. For example, if you meet someone who says 'Hi! I'm Carlos,' don't just say 'Hello.' Repeat the person's name. Say 'Hello, Carlos.'

* If you have to remember something that's big, break it into smaller sections. For example, it's hard to memorise 109244153. But if you break it into three sections – 109 / 244 / 153 – it becomes easier.

* Always review information. If you bring things you've learned back to your mind, they become more memorable. For example, before you go to sleep it's a good idea to remind yourself of the new things you learned that day. They'll be easier to remember the next day.

* Relax – nothing is easy to learn if you're stressed.

* Above all, never tell yourself that you have a bad memory. You can always do something to help improve your memory, and everyone's memory gets better if they use it often enough.

c 🔊 Read the text again and listen. Mark the statements *T* (true) or *F* (false).

1 The human brain can't hold as much information as a computer. ☐

2 Computers can't remember things as well as humans can. ☐

3 Different people are good at remembering different things. ☐

4 Mozart's brain was excellent, but there were things that he did not remember at all. ☐

5 If you often forget things, there is nothing you can do to improve your memory. ☐

6 You will remember information more easily if you revise it. ☐

2 Grammar

Determiners
(*everyone, no one, someone* etc.)

a Look at the examples. Find other examples of determiners in the text on page 74 and underline them.

*No one remembers **everything**.*

*Here are some tips. **All of them** are helpful, but **none of them** can make your memory 100% perfect.*

b Complete the words in the chart. Use the text on page 74 to help you.

....	something	....
everyone	....	....
everywhere	somewhere	nowhere
....	some of them	....

c Write the correct words in the spaces. Choose from the words in the box.

> ~~Someone~~   everyone   everywhere
> all of them   everything   none of them
> no one

1   *Someone* gave me this book for my birthday, but I can't remember who it was.

2   I rang your place four times this morning, but .... answered.

3   *Use Your Memory* by Tony Buzan is a brilliant book. I think .... should read it.

4   It was a hard question. She asked all her friends, but .... knew the answer.

5   I can remember .... our teacher said in today's lesson, but I can't remember what the homework is!

6   Jim's lost his watch! He's looked .... for it, but he can't find it.

7   My dad doesn't see his friends from London very often. That's why he was very happy that .... came to his party.

Look

In English there are no double negatives. Look at these examples.

*I know **nothing** about Mozart.*
*I **don't** know **anything** about Mozart.*
(Not: ~~I don't know nothing about Mozart.~~)

3 Vocabulary

Remembering and forgetting

a Look at these words from the text on page 74. How do you say them in your language?

to **remember** (something)
to **forget** (something)
a (good/bad) **memory**
to **memorise** (something)
to **remind** (someone to do something)
a **memorable** (name)

b (Circle) the correct words.

1   I'll never *forget / remember* the time we had in Greece – it was a really *memorable / remind* holiday!

2   I promise I won't *forget / remind* my homework tomorrow.

3   **A:** John! Please don't *remember / forget* to switch off the light.

   B: Dad! Don't *remind / remember* me every day! I always *remind / remember* to switch it off.

4   My dad's got a really bad *memorable / memory*. I always have to *remember / remind* him to give me my pocket money.

5   In the first 15 minutes of the lesson, our new teacher *reminded / memorised* everyone's names!

c Work with a partner. Ask and answer these questions.

1   Are there any things you always remember or forget?

2   Do people often have to remind you to do things?

3   When you need to memorise information, how do you do it? (For example, write it down several times, read it aloud etc.)

4 Listen

a 🔊 What do Albert Einstein and Tom Cruise have in common? Listen to an interview with a psychologist, Dr Jane Cairns, to check your ideas.

Albert Einstein

Tom Cruise

b 🔊 Listen again and answer the questions.

1 When did Einstein learn to speak and read?

2 How does Tom Cruise learn his lines? Why?

3 Did Einstein's teachers think he was intelligent? Why / Why not?

4 When and how did Einstein first get his ideas about space and time?

c 🔊 In the second part of the interview, Dr Cairns talks about different 'intelligences'. Look at these six examples of types of 'intelligence' in the box below. Complete the sentences with the types of intelligence. Then listen to the second part of the interview and check your answers.

logical-mathematical intelligence

verbal intelligence

musical intelligence

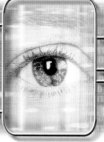

visual intelligence

body intelligence

interpersonal intelligence

1 People with high *logical-mathematical intelligence* are often good at Maths and finding answers to problems.

2 If you have high .... you are probably good at movement, for example sports and dancing.

3 If you have a lot of .... you are probably good at painting and drawing.

4 If you have a lot of .... you are probably good at understanding other people and working with them.

5 People with high .... are often good at singing or playing a musical instrument.

6 People with good .... are usually good speakers and like words.

5 Speak

What's your strongest intelligence?

a Do you remember things best by seeing, feeling or hearing? Try a fun test. Listen to your teacher's instructions.

b In which of the tests did you get the best result? If you remembered most numbers in test one, it means you probably have a good visual memory. If you scored well in test two, you probably remember things best if you've heard them. If you did well in test three perhaps you learn best when you feel or do things.

6 Grammar
must/mustn't vs. don't have to

a Read Lisa's letter to a problem page and the replies. What's her problem? Which reply do you like most? Why?

Dear Claire

I get bad grades at school, especially in Maths. My dad says I must try harder, because he wants me to go to university. He thinks I'm lazy, but it's not true, I work really hard! I've tried to talk to my mother – but she says I have to work as hard as my brother does. But my brother doesn't have to study hard and he always gets excellent grades. It's not fair!

The only thing I like is Art. My teacher says I'm the best student she's had for years. When I told my dad, all he said was, 'You mustn't waste your time on Art and you must work harder!' Please help me, I don't know what to do!

Lisa, Birmingham

Dear Lisa

You mustn't think that your parents are wrong and you're right. Remember that you're younger than they are and they want the best for you. So you must listen to your parents and try harder.

Claire

Dear Lisa

Please remember that your future is very important. You don't have to do everything your parents tell you to do, and you mustn't worry too much about Maths – you don't have to be good at everything! Talk to your parents again and try not to get angry this time.

Claire

b Look at the examples. <u>Underline</u> more examples of *must*, *mustn't* and *don't/doesn't have to* in the texts. Then complete the rule.

*My dad says I **must** try harder.*
*You **mustn't** think that your parents are wrong.*
*My brother **doesn't have to** study hard.*

Rule:
- Use _____ (n't) to give someone strong advice or for expressing strong obligations.
- Use _____ to say that something is <u>not</u> necessary.

c (Circle) the correct words.

1
You can go out tonight, but you *mustn't / don't have to* come home later than 1 am.

2
UNDER 12 - FREE
Great! I'm under 12! I *mustn't / don't have to* pay!

3
Great! No school today – I don't *have to / mustn't* get up early.
7:00

4
OK, you can keep it – but it *mustn't / doesn't have to* leave this room!

d Complete the sentences with *must*, *mustn't*, or *don't have to*.

1 I *mustn't* forget to send my grandmother a birthday card!
2 You really _____ see that film! It's great!
3 My parents _____ go to work tomorrow because it's a public holiday.
4 You _____ remember to do your homework. You always forget!
5 My sister _____ go to school yet because she's only three!
6 Hurry up! We _____ be late again.

7 Pronunciation
must

🔊 Turn to page 121.

The winners are ...

8 Read and listen

a 🔊 Where are the people in the story? Why do you think Joanne looks unhappy in picture 3? Who do you think Amy's talking to in picture 4? Read, listen and check your answers.

1

Matt: So – this is it. We're first. Is everybody ready?

Dave: Yeah. Are you OK, Amy?

Amy: Yes, you don't have to worry about me. I'm fine.

Joanne: OK, they're calling us. Come on – I'll go first!

2

Matt: Oh no – perhaps she was nervous, I hope Amy sings better than that!

Dave: Yeah, me too!

Announcer: For their next song we have Amy singing *April*.

3

Joanne: They don't know good singing when they hear it!

Matt: Mmm, maybe.

Announcer: And the winners are: from Leeds, Saints Alive!

An hour later...

4

Joanne: What a terrible result! Not even third!

Dave: Never mind. There's always next time. We mustn't give up, must we?

Matt: We just need to practise a bit more, that's all. Where's Amy?

Joanne: Look – she's talking to some blokes over there. Are they her mates?

Dave: No, look – they're the blokes from the band that won.

Matt: They were wicked!

Dave: Yeah – but I wonder why they're talking to Amy?

b Mark the sentences *T* (true), *F* (false) or *N* (not enough information).

1 Matt is nervous about going on to the stage. `N`

2 Joanne wants to be first on to the stage.

3 Amy thinks she sang well.

4 Joanne thinks she didn't sing well.

5 Dave's band comes fifth in the contest.

6 Joanne doesn't know who Amy is talking to.

7 Dave knows what the boys are talking to Amy about.

9 Everyday English

(a) Find expressions 1–4 from the story. Who says them? Match them with definitions a–d.

1 <u>Come on.</u>
2 <u>Never mind.</u>
3 Are they her <u>mates</u>?
4 I <u>wonder</u> why.

a I don't know
b friends
c Let's go
d Don't worry about it

(b) Complete the sentences with the <u>underlined</u> words from Exercise 9a.

1 Jane: It's awful – I only got 10% in Geography!
   Klara: _____ , Jane. You got 75% in Maths, didn't you?

2 Marek: Do you know that girl over there?
   Sylvie: Yes – that's Anna, she's one of my best _____ . I've known her for year!

3 Jan: I _____ where Maria is. I haven't seen her since last night.
   Markus: I saw her this morning, but I think she's gone home now.

4 Josh: What time is it, Harry?
   Harry: Half past eight – and the match starts at nine! _____ – we're late!

10 Write

(a) You have decided to enter an English writing competition. Read the advertisement for the competition. What do you have to do?

(b) Read Frances' entry to the competition. What are her answers to the questions in the advertisement?

Competition!

Write in English ...
... and win a prize!

Write a composition of about 120–150 words on the following topic:

● What are the things you are really good at (in school and in your free time)?

● What things are you <u>not</u> very good at?

● Why do you think you are good / not good at these things?

● What kind of job would you like to do in the future? Why?

I think I've got good 'body intelligence' because I'm quite good at swimming, for example, and I love dancing. At school, my best subjects are Maths and Art. I enjoy doing Maths problems, and I love painting, so perhaps I've got good visual and logical intelligence, too!

I'm not very good at languages – it's difficult for me to memorise new words and to understand the grammar. I don't get very good marks, but I don't have to be good at everything.

When I finish school, I'd like to be an architect. I think I could be good at this job because I am good at Maths, and because I like drawing things and design. Also, architects don't have to speak a foreign language!

Frances Mason

(c) Now write your answer for the competition. Use the advertisement and Frances' entry to help you.

12 Music makers

✳ Present perfect continuous / present perfect simple and continuous
✳ Vocabulary: music

1 Read and listen

(a) How old do you think the girl in the photo is? Why do you think she's a 'young winner'? Read the magazine article quickly to check your ideas.

(b) 🔊 Read the article again and listen. Answer the questions.

1 What does Jennifer's father do?
2 When did Jennifer start playing the violin?
3 Was Jennifer surprised when she won the Young Musician of the Year competition?
4 Why have people been phoning Jennifer?
5 What are some of Jennifer's other interests?

(c) Jennifer says, 'I'm quite normal.' Do you agree? Why / Why not?

A Young Winner

Do you think classical music is only for old people? Then you probably haven't heard of sensational violinist **Jennifer Pike**. In 2002, Jennifer won the BBC television's *Young Musician of the Year* competition – aged only twelve.

Where is she from?

Jennifer is from Cheshire, in the north of England. She lives there with her family, and she goes to a school in Manchester, where her father has been teaching music for many years. She's got a sister, Alexandra, who is three years older.

How long has she been playing the violin?

Jennifer has been playing the violin since she was five years old. Her father gave her a violin and he knew immediately that she was special. He says, 'She wasn't afraid of the instrument. She is a completely natural player. I've been teaching young musicians for years, but this is something different.'

How did she feel when she became Young Musician of the Year?

She says: 'It was amazing, I really didn't think I would win. I still can't believe it – sometimes I think I've been dreaming, and in a minute I'll wake up!'

Jennifer is well-known now – does that bring problems?

'The phone has been ringing non-stop!' says her father. 'People all over the world have invited her to play in concerts. But we think she'll have to say "No". She's played in a lot of concerts this year but school's important too and she has exams.'

Classical music is important in Jennifer's life. Does she have other interests?

'Oh yes, lots!' she says. 'For example, I like pop music too – I like Robbie Williams a lot! Also, I've been playing tennis for years, and table tennis. I love swimming too. I'd like to play basketball, but I can't because of my hands. What else? Well, I like lying in bed in the morning, and text messaging my friends. I'm quite normal!'

2 Grammar

Present perfect continuous

a Look at the examples.

*... her father **has been teaching** music for many years.*
*I've **been playing tennis** for years.*

b <u>Underline</u> other examples of the present perfect continuous in the text on page 80. Then complete the table and the rule.

Positive	Negative	Question	Short answer
I/you/we/they **'ve (have) been** working.	I/you/we/they .... working.	**Have** I/you/we/they been working?	Yes, I/you/we/they/ .... No, I/you/we/they/ ....
He/she/it .... working.	He/she/it **hasn't (has not) been** working.	.... he/she/it .... working?	Yes, he/she/it .... No, he/she/it/ ....

c Look at the pictures. Write a sentence in the present perfect continuous for each picture.

1 She / run.
She's been running .

2 He / cook all morning.
--- .

3 I / not feel well.
--- .

4 You / not practise enough!
--- !

5 They / play football.
--- .

6 We / watch too much TV!
--- !

Rule:

Use the present perfect continuous to:

● talk about situations which started in the .... and are still continuing now.

  Example: *I've been teaching for years.*

● talk about actions that have just stopped and may have a result in the present.

  Example: *I'm hot* because *I've been running.*

● focus on how long an activity has been in progress. The activity may or may not be complete.

  Example: *I've been writing emails* all morning.

d Write complete sentences. Use the present perfect continuous.

1 How long / she / play / the violin? *How long has she been playing the violin?*

2 I / wait / a long time / for you! ....

3 He / not sleep / enough.
----

4 What / you / do / this morning? ....

5 I / not learn / English / very long. ....

6 How long / you / eat?
----

7 They / do their homework / for three hours. ....

8 How long / we / walk?
----

3 Pronunciation

Sentence stress: rhythm

🔊 Turn to page 121.

4 Grammar

Present perfect continuous and present perfect simple

a) Look at the examples. Then complete the rule.

*Jennifer **has been playing** the violin since she was five years old.*
***She's played** in a lot of concerts this year.*

> **Rule:**
> - Use the _____ tense, not the _____ tense to show that an action is now completed.
>   **Example:** *I've been to Italy.*
> - Use the _____ , not the _____ , to stress the <u>finished result</u> of a completed activity and the <u>amount</u> we have completed.
>   **Example:** *I've written <u>three emails</u> this morning.*

Look

Some verbs are not usually used in continuous tenses.

I've known Annie for a long time.
(Not: ~~I've been knowing ...~~)

I've never understood John.
(Not: ~~I've never been understanding ...~~)

b) Circle the correct words.

1 She's *written* / *been writing* three letters this afternoon.
2 I've *read* / *been reading* this page four times and I still don't understand it all!
3 He's in hospital because *he's had* / *he's been having* an accident.
4 Ouch! I've *cut* / *been cutting* my finger!
5 My mother's making sandwiches – she's *cut* / *been cutting* bread all morning.
6 Great news! You've *won* / *been winning* the competition!
7 James *has known* / *has been knowing* his wife since he was a child.

c) Complete the sentences. Use the present perfect continuous or the present perfect simple forms of the verbs.

1 I *have been studying* (study) for my test since I got up.
2 _____ you _____ (not finish) that book yet?
3 He looks terrible! What _____ he _____ (do) all night?
4 _____ that singer _____ (make) any CDs yet?
5 I'm sorry, I _____ (not start) my homework yet.
6 My brother works really hard when he wants to. He _____ (clean) four rooms this morning!
7 It _____ (rain) for days – will it ever stop?

5 Speak

a) Read about the pop star, David Bowie.

David Bowie was born in 1947. He learned to play the saxophone, and then became a singer. He makes records, and he is also an actor in films. He is married to a model called Iman.

b) Work with a partner. Student A: read the information about David Bowie on this page. Student B: turn to page 123. Ask and answer questions to complete your missing information. Student A: you start.

A: *How long has he been singing?*

> **David Bowie**
> - He / sing/ for _____ years. (*How long _____ ?*)
> - He / play saxophone for more than 40 years.
> - He / make / records / (*How long _____ ?.*
> - He / make / more than five films.
> - He / marry to Iman / _____ years.

6 Vocabulary
Music

(a) 🔊 Listen to the music extracts and write the words from the box next to numbers 1–6.

> country   reggae   jazz   folk   heavy metal   classical

1 ....   2 ....   3 ....   4 ....   5 ....   6 ....

(b) 🔊 Match the words with the pictures. Write the names of the instruments from the box in the spaces. Then listen, check and repeat.

> a piano   drums   a trumpet   a violin   a clarinet
> an electric guitar   a saxophone   a flute   synthesiser   keyboards

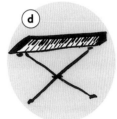

....

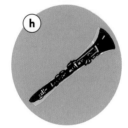

....

(c) What's the difference between: *live* music and *recorded* music? An *album* and a *single*? A *hi-fi* and a *personal stereo*?

7 Listen

🔊 Listen to four people talking about music and instruments. Complete the information in the table.

	Musical instrument	Time spent playing / learning	Favourite type(s) of music	Favourite way of listening to music
1 Tom	*saxophone*	....	....	....
2 Alice	....	....	....	....
3 Phil	....	....	....	....
4 Vanessa	....	....	....	....

8 Speak

Work with a partner. Ask and answer the questions.

- Does anyone in your family play a musical instrument? How long has he/she been playing?
- Do you play a musical instrument? If yes, how long have you been playing? If not, would you like to? Which instrument(s) would you like to play?
- What's your favourite kind of music? Who are your favourite bands/singers?
- How often do you listen to music?
- How do you like listening to music? (On the radio? Personal stereo ...?)

Culture in mind

9 Read

(a) Look at the pictures and the decades in the box. Match each picture to one of the decades. Write a–e in the boxes. Then read the magazine article to check your ideas.

1950s ☐   1960s ☐   1970s ☐   1980s ☐   1990s ☐

POP MUSIC
IN BRITAIN AND THE USA
A BRIEF HISTORY

THE 1950s

This was the decade that rock 'n' roll really started in the USA, with singers like Chuck Berry and Elvis Presley, and bands like Bill Haley and the Comets. There were some amazing haircuts, too!

THE 1960s

In Britain, this was the decade of the Beatles and the Rolling Stones. In America, the Beach Boys (surf music) and Bob Dylan ('protest' folk music) were huge. Other big names in the UK were Pink Floyd and Cream, and in the USA, The Doors, Jefferson Airplane and the Grateful Dead. This was the hippy period – men often wore their hair long, and flared jeans and 'psychedelic' shirts and jackets were popular.

THE 1970s

In Britain, punk rock began with the Sex Pistols. Many teenagers had brightly coloured hair and piercings. Heavy metal started up, with bands like Aerosmith, AC/DC and Kiss. The 1970s were also the period of the first 100% electronically produced disco music.

THE 1980s

Bands like U2 and REM started in the 1980s. Then hip hop completely changed the music scene with bands like The Beastie Boys and Public Enemy. Orchestral Manoeuvres In The Dark played synth-pop, which was music played on electronic instruments called synthesisers. Depeche Mode and the Pet Shop Boys were very successful at this time.

THE 1990s

Techno music was started by DJs in the USA, where rock music was still popular. Brit pop was played by two successful bands, Blur and Oasis, who shared the number one spot for years. Rave, house, trip hop, garage music – all different kinds of dance music – made their way into British parties. Boy bands and girl bands like The Backstreet Boys, The Spice Girls and 'N Sync started to appear.

THE EARLY 2000s

Boy bands continue to do well, and Robbie Williams' style of music makes him a hit. Indie music is played by guitar bands like Travis and Coldplay, and solo singers like Britney Spears and Jennifer Lopez have become very popular.

b Answer the questions.

1. In which country did rock 'n' roll start?
2. In which decade did men start to have long hair?
3. What was special about disco music in the 1970s?
4. How did synth-pop get its name?
5. Who started techno music, and where?

Discussion box

Work in pairs or small groups. Discuss these questions together.

1. Do you know any of the groups or singers in the text? What do you know about them?
2. How would *you* complete the paragraph for the 2000s?
3. Look at the pictures again. What do you think of the fashions since the 1950s? Which decade's fashions do you prefer?

10 Write

a Read this part of a letter Jenny wrote to her friend, Sandy. What kind of information does she want?

In your next letter, please tell me:
• what kind of music you like and how long you've liked it.
• who your favourite bands and singers are. Why do you like them?
• do you spend a lot of time listening to music, and how do you prefer to listen?

Looking forward to hearing from you.

b Read Sandy's reply to Jenny and answer the questions in Exercise 10a.

A Hi Jenny,

Thanks for your letter. I'm happy to tell you what you wanted to know – I'm mad about music! My favourite is country music. I've been a country music fan for two years, since I heard Shania Twain on the radio – she's great! I think her best song is 'You're Still the One'.

B Some of my friends think I'm strange – they listen to bands like Sive and The Backstreet Boys. They're OK of course, but I prefer listening to Garth Brooks and Brian Landrie. I spend nearly all my money on country CDs. I've got lots of CDs by Meredith Edwards and Jessica Andrews, too. I like country music because the singers have got great voices and the lyrics are usually good too. Some people think that country music's all the same, but they're wrong! There are lots of different kinds of songs – romantic ones, slow ones, fast ones – just like any other kind of music.

C I listen to country music nearly all the time. I usually listen on headphones in my bedroom, but sometimes my friends come round to my place and we listen together on the CD player.

Please write to me again soon. Love, Sandy.

c Write a letter about your favourite type of music. Organise your writing into paragraphs. Use Jenny's questions and Sandy's answer to help you.

For your portfolio

Module 3 Check your progress

1 Grammar

a) Complete the sentences. Use the past simple passive form of the verbs.

1 The Statue of Liberty *was built* (build) in France.

2 It was a terrible accident. How many people .... (kill)?

3 Last week I .... (invite) to a party, but I couldn't go.

4 We didn't play well yesterday. We .... (beat) 4–0!

5 When the volcano erupted, the noise .... (hear) 200 kilometres away.

6 Tomas fell off his bike yesterday, but he .... (not injure).

7 The houses .... (damage) in the earthquake, but luckily they .... (not destroy). |6|

b) Complete the sentences with *a*, *an* or *the*.

My grandparents live in ¹*an* old cottage in the countryside. It's got ² .... bedroom, ³ .... bathroom, ⁴ .... living room and ⁵ .... kitchen. ⁶ .... bedroom and ⁷ .... living room are quite big, but ⁸ .... kitchen's very small! |7|

c) Complete the sentences with *too much / too many* or *not (n't) enough*.

1 There's nowhere to sit – there are *n't enough* chairs here!

2 I was still hungry after the party because there was .... food there.

3 I couldn't finish the test because there was .... time.

4 We couldn't dance because there were .... people in the room.

5 I feel sick – I think I've eaten .... chocolate!

6 I didn't really like my visit to Rome last summer because there were .... tourists everywhere.

7 There are .... places to go in my town – it's really boring! |6|

d) Complete the sentences with *will* or *going to*.

1 Next summer we *'re going* (go) to Spain for our holiday. We've booked the flights.

2 I've put some old clothes on because I .... (wash) my dad's car for him.

3 What time .... we .... (meet) John this evening?

4 Please can you lend me some money? I promise I .... (pay) you back on Friday.

5 I'm sorry, Josh can't come to school tomorrow. He .... (visit) his grandmother in hospital.

6 I'm afraid I lost your book – I .... (buy) you another one tomorrow.

7 Julie has already thought of a present for Susie – she .... (give) her a DVD.

8 Give me that bag. I .... (carry) it for you. |7|

e) Complete the sentences with the words in the box.

~~everyone~~   everything   no one   nothing
none of them   someone   somewhere

1 I think the *Star Wars* films are great – *everyone* should go and see them!

2 I'm bored – I've got .... to do!

3 This morning .... gave me a present, but I have no idea who it was!

4 I was really happy in the English lesson because I understood .... the teacher said.

5 I put my magazine .... , but now I can't find it!

6 He found lots of shirts in the shop, but .... were the colour he wanted.

7 I told a great joke this morning but .... laughed! I don't think they understood it. |6|

f) Complete the sentences with *mustn't* or *don't / doesn't have to*.

1 Tomorrow's a holiday, so we *don't have to* go to school.

2 I understand – you .... explain everything again.

3 You .... eat in class – it's a school rule.

4 Hurry up, Sally – we .... miss the bus again!

5 My sister's revising for her exams, so she .... do any housework.

6 Mum and Dad told us we .... get home later than midnight. |5|

g (Circle) the correct words.

1 I've (drunk)/ been drinking four cups of coffee this morning!
2 I'm really happy – my aunt has sent / been sending me some money for my birthday.
3 My brother has talked / been talking on the phone all morning.
4 The dog's really dirty because he's played / been playing in the garden.
5 My parents have visited / been visiting my grandparents three times this month.
6 I've read / been reading this book since ten o'clock, but I still haven't finished / been finishing it.

[ ] 5

2 Vocabulary

a (Circle) the words to find two types of homes, four musical instruments and four types of music. (➤ or ▼)

D	V	I	O	L	I	N	A	Z	Z	T	O
E	I	X	R	E	G	G	A	E	A	R	S
T	O	M	B	O	N	E	T	G	H	U	E
A	J	A	Z	Z	C	A	R	A	R	M	P
C	B	U	N	A	E	L	O	W	B	P	I
H	U	G	G	G	A	A	C	T	I	E	A
E	N	U	A	F	R	F	O	L	K	T	N
D	G	I	L	D	D	S	U	N	K	C	T
F	A	T	L	I	E	S	N	E	J	A	Z
C	L	A	R	I	N	E	T	T	E	R	R
F	O	R	E	T	E	R	R	A	C	E	D
O	W	R	O	N	F	T	Y	D	E	Q	U

[ ] 10

b Underline the odd one out.

1 gate   chimney   garage   <u>neighbours</u>
2 remind   remember   memory   forget
3 bungalow   garage   cottage   flat
4 flood   earthquake   avalanche   bomb
5 pop   rock   classical   keyboards
6 saxophone   guitar   flute   trumpet
7 TV aerial   semi-detached   chimney   gate

[ ] 6

c Complete the sentences. Use one of the words from the box in each space.

> remember   forget   ~~memory~~   memorise
> remind   memorable

1 I've got a very good _memory_ for numbers.
2 We had a lovely time last Saturday – it was great, a really _____ day.
3 Please don't _____ to take the dog out.
4 I know his face, but I can't _____ his name!
5 John, can you _____ your brother that we're going out tonight?
6 For our homework tonight, we have to _____ a long text in French.

[ ] 5

3 Everyday English

a Complete the dialogue with the words in the box.

> ~~what's up with~~   get rid of   got a point
> sort of   never mind   mates

Mike: Your sister looks very unhappy.
¹ _What's up with_ her?

Clare: She's angry with me. She thinks I was rude to her ² _____ .

Mike: Oh? And were you rude to them?

Clare: Well, ³ _____ . I told them to go away. They were noisy and I was trying to work. I wanted to ⁴ _____ them!

Mike: Well, that was a bit rude. Perhaps your sister's ⁵ _____ !

Clare: Mike – it was nothing!

Mike: Well, ⁶ _____ , she'll be OK tomorrow.

[ ] 5

How did you do?

Tick (✓) a box for each section.

Total score	😊 Very good	😐 OK	😞 Not very good
[ ] 68			
Grammar	32 – 42	26 – 31	less than 26
Vocabulary	17 – 21	12 – 16	less than 12
Everyday English	4 – 5	3	less than 3

Module 4
Dreams and reality

YOU WILL LEARN ABOUT ...

- Medicine in the past ....
- A girl who started a website ....
- Some of the problems computers can cause ....
- The discovery of an ancient Inca city ....
- An ancient terracotta army in China ....
- A shoeshine boy who became a film star ....
- The history of some superstitions ....

  ✱ Can you match each picture with a topic?

YOU WILL LEARN HOW TO ...

Speak

- Ask and answer questions about your childhood habits
- Give advice
- Ask and answer questions about imaginary situations
- Talk about computers and the Internet
- Tell a picture story
- Report statements and questions
- Discuss superstitions

Write

- An article about a famous doctor or scientist
- A competition entry for a computer magazine
- A story about something you found
- An email to apologise to a friend

Read

- An article about medicine in the past
- A text about how teenagers use computers
- An article about a website entrepreneur
- A text about problems computers can cause
- An article about the discovery of Machu Picchu
- A story about a shoeshine boy

Listen

- Dialogues at the doctor's
- A conversation about Joseph Lister
- People talking about computers
- A radio interview about a terracotta army

Use grammar

Can you match the names of the grammar points with the examples?

Defining relative clauses	My father **asked me why I was** late.
used to	When I was young, I **used to cry** a lot.
Second conditional	He **told me he would write** to me.
Past perfect	I **would have invited** her **if I'd seen** her.
Reported statements	My bike wasn't there – someone **had stolen** it!
Reported questions	That's the shop **where** I bought this shirt.
Third conditional	**If I knew**, I'd **tell** you.

Use vocabulary

Can you think of two more examples for each topic?

Medicine	Computer technology	Noun suffixes -r, -er, -or and -ist	Noun suffixes -ation and -ment
doctor	computer	driv**er**	educ**ation**
treatment	website	art**ist**	improve**ment**
....	....	....	....
....	....	....	....

13 Doctor's orders

* Defining relative clauses
* *used to*
* Vocabulary: medicine

1 Read and listen

a Which of these things in the pictures do you think people in the past did to treat headaches? Read the text to check your ideas.

make a hole in the patient's head

hold the patient's head under water

tie a ceramic crocodile to the patient's head

put leeches on the patient's neck

Medicine in the past – treating headaches

People have always had headaches. They are a common health problem that people have all over the world. In some cultures people use special herbs. For example, Native American Indians use plants which contain a chemical found in aspirins. But today, most people in the developed world take a tablet to treat a headache – aspirin, for example. In the past, however, people didn't use to have tablets, so what did they use to do?

Many years ago, headaches were treated in all kinds of ways – and some of the treatments might be hard for us to believe in the twenty-first century! Thousands of years ago, for example, medicine men used to make holes in the heads of people with headaches, because they believed this would let the headache out. This may seem very cruel to us, but in those days people believed this treatment would make their headache go away.

In ancient Egypt, medicine men had a different way of treating headaches. They used to tie a ceramic crocodile, which was filled with herbs, to the head of the patient. The reasons for this are not clear to us today.

In the Middle Ages, there were no hospitals and only people who were rich could afford to go to doctors. But the people that did go to doctors were usually treated with leeches – small, black creatures that suck blood. They were put on the patient's body near the place where the pain was. For people who had headaches, the leech was usually put on the neck.

These treatments were probably quite painful, and they may seem very strange to us now. Just imagine what dentists used to do to people that had toothache!

b 🔊 Read the text again and listen. Mark the sentences *T* (true), *F* (false) or *N* (not enough information).

1 Native Americans never take tablets for headaches. ☐
2 Medicine men made holes in people's heads because they wanted to hurt them. ☐
3 We are not sure why ceramic crocodiles were used to treat headaches. ☐
4 In the Middle Ages, doctors were very rich. ☐
5 Leeches were put on people's heads to stop headaches. ☐

c Do you know of any other unusual ways people used to treat illnesses in the past, or ways that are used today?

2 Grammar

Defining relative clauses

a Look at these example. Find more examples of defining relative clauses in the text on page 90 and <u>underline</u> them. Then complete the rule.

*Only **people who were rich** could afford to go to doctors.*
*They were put on the patient's body near the **place where the pain** was.*

b (Circle) the correct word.

1 The tablets ⟨that⟩ / where are used here cost a lot of money!
2 The nurse which / who saw me was very nice.
3 That's the office that / where my mother used to work.
4 Most people don't like doctors who / where don't smile.
5 There's a girl in my class which / who gets terrible headaches.
6 The books that / who are on my list aren't in the library.
7 At lunchtime, I always go to a quiet room where / which I can relax.

Rule:

● Use defining relative clauses to make it clear exactly who, or what, you are talking about.

● Use _____ or *that* for people.

● Use _____ or _____ for things and animals.

● Use _____ for places.

3 Vocabulary and listening

Medicine

a Match the parts of the sentences to complete the definitions.

1 A doctor is someone who   takes people to hospital.
2 A hospital is a place where   has a health problem.
3 A patient is someone who   you take with water to make you better.
4 A dentist is someone that   tries to make sick people better.
5 A tablet is something which   doctors and nurses work.
6 An ambulance is a vehicle that   you visit if you have a problem with your teeth.

b 🔊 Match the pictures and the sentences. Write the letters in the boxes. Then listen, check and repeat.

a 'I've got toothache.'
b 'I've got stomach ache.'
c 'My eyes hurt.'
d 'I've got a temperature.'
e 'I've got a sore throat.'
f 'My ankle hurts.'
g 'I've got a cold.'
h 'I've got a pain in my chest.'

c 🔊 Listen to four patients at the doctor's. What problem does each person have?

4 Grammar

used to

a Look at these examples from the text on page 90.

*In the past, people **didn't use to** have tablets – so what **did they use to** do?*
*Just imagine what dentists **used to do** to people that had toothache!*

b Look at these sentences. Can you explain the difference?

*I **used to listen** to ABBA songs a lot when I was ten.*

*I **listened** to the new Mariah Carey song this morning. I think it's great.*

c Complete the table and the rule.

Positive	Negative	Question	Short answer
I/you/we/they/he/she/it .... live in London.	I/you/we/they/he/she/it they **didn't use to** live in London.	.... I/you/we/they/he/she/it .... to live in London?	Yes, I/you/we/they/he/she/it .... No, I/you/we/they/he/she/it ....

Rule: *used to* + verb expresses an action which happened regularly in the .... but doesn't happen ....

d Match sentences 1–5 with sentences a–e.

1 Jane used to eat lots of hamburgers.
2 Karen used to read lots of comics.
3 We often used to go to our flat on the beach.
4 Tony and I used to play table tennis.
5 We used to go to Greece for our holidays.

a She reads teenage magazines now.
b He still plays twice a week, but I don't play any more.
c We don't go there any more. We prefer Italy now.
d She stopped eating fast food a year ago.
e We sold it a year ago and bought a bigger flat in town.

e Complete the sentences. Use the present simple and the correct form of *used to*.

1 That shop *used to be* (be) a clothes shop, but now it *sells* (sell) CDs.
2 You .... (be) my friend, but now you only .... (say) horrible things about me!
3 We .... (live) in a small flat in the city, but we .... (not live) there any more.
4 His father .... (not smoke) any more, but when he was younger he .... (smoke) sixty cigarettes a day!
5 My favourite player .... (not be) very good now, but he .... (be) the best in the country.
6 I .... (not listen) to reggae when I was younger, but now I .... (love) it!
7 A: .... (you/like) eggs when you were a child?
   B: No, but now I .... (love) them.
8 A: .... (your father/play) football when he was younger?
   B: Yes he did – but he .... (be) too old now!

5 Pronunciation

/z/ or /s/ in *used*

🔊 Turn to page 121.

6 Speak

a Work in pairs. Student A: look at the information here. Student B: turn to page 123. Think about when you were five or six years old. Read each question and tick (✓) the box if it is true for you. Put a cross (✗) if it is not true.

When you were small, did you use to ...?

	YOU	YOUR FRIEND
1 ... like vegetables?	☐	☐
2 ... read comics?	☐	☐
3 ... watch cartoons on TV?	☐	☐
4 ... help with housework?	☐	☐
5 ... listen to music in your bedroom?	☐	☐
6 ... be afraid of monsters?	☐	☐

b Now ask Student B about him/her, for example:

When I was small, I didn't use to like vegetables. Did you?

Put a tick (✓) or cross (✗) in the boxes under 'your friend'.

7 Listen

a Joseph Lister was the man who first used antiseptics. What are antiseptics used for?

b 🔊 Listen to Vicky telling Andy about a programme she saw about Joseph Lister. Why did a lot of patients use to die in hospitals?

c 🔊 Read the summary and try to complete it with the missing words. Then listen again and check your answers.

Joseph Lister

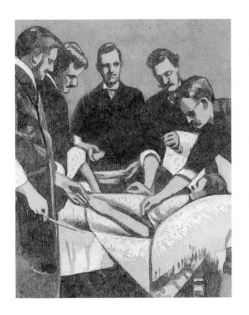

Joseph Lister was a doctor from [1]_____ . He lived in the [2]_____ century and was the first doctor to use antiseptics in [3]_____ . In those days, hospitals used to be really [4]_____ and so a lot of patients used to [5]_____ . Doctors didn't use to [6]_____ their hands before they treated patients. In the city hospital where Lister worked, a lot of people were [7]_____ , so he decided to tell all the [8]_____ to wash their hands. But even after this, [9]_____% of the patients died. Later, he started to use [10]_____ to clean all the medical instruments and after that, only [11]_____% of the patients died. At first, other doctors laughed at Lister, but in the end they realised that he was [12]_____ .

I used to like Joanne

8 Read and listen

a 🔊 Look at the photo and the title. Who do you think Amy was talking to after the contest? What do you think will happen next? Read, listen and check your answers.

Joanne: It's awful! We practised for weeks, and we've ended up with nothing!

Matt: True. But we've got the experience now, and we can try again next year.

Dave: Only if we hang on to Amy.

Joanne: What? You're kidding!

Dave: No, I'm not. Look, tonight the crowd loved Amy, and I think the blokes from Saints Alive did, too.

Joanne: Oh look – here comes super-girl now!

Amy: Hi, you guys. Sorry I'm late. I was talking to some people.

Dave: Yeah, we know – the blokes in the band that won. What did they want?

Amy: They want me to join them. They need a girl singer.

Matt: Wow! And they won the contest – so you might make a record!

Amy: Yeah! Cool, eh!

Dave: So what did you say to them, Amy?

Amy: I said I'll think about it. I'm seeing them again tomorrow afternoon, we're going to Josh's place to practise. He's the guy who plays guitar.

Matt: That's great. Congratulations!

Dave: Yeah. You know, you sang really well.

Matt: Yeah, you were great. Wasn't she, Joanne?

Joanne: Yes, well done. Look, I'm off now. I'll see you some time – maybe.

Amy: Bye, Joanne.

Dave: You know, I used to like Joanne, but now ...

b Answer the questions.

1 Who wants to keep Amy in the band?
2 Who *doesn't* want to keep Amy in the band?
3 What do the boys in the other band want Amy to do?
4 What did Amy say to them?
5 How do Dave and Matt feel about Amy's news?
6 How does Joanne feel about Amy's news?
7 How does Dave feel about Joanne now?

9 Everyday English

(a) Find expressions 1–4 in the story. Who says them? Match them with definitions a–d.

1 we've <u>ended up with</u>   a well done
2 <u>hang on to</u>   b finally got
3 <u>You're kidding!</u>   c keep
4 <u>Congratulations!</u>   d you're joking

(b) Complete the sentences with the <u>underlined</u> words from Exercise 9a.

1 Suzie: I won the tennis competition at school!
   Ben: Really? That's great. .... !
2 Laura: Steve's going out with Jacky now.
   Diana: What? .... ! Jacky's always hated Steve!
3 These old books are worth a lot of money now, so I'm going to .... them.
4 I bought a lot of clothes and CDs yesterday, and I've .... only two pounds in my pocket!

10 Write

(a) Dave wrote an article for homework about a famous person. He chose Marie Curie. Read his notes and the article he wrote. How did Marie Curie become famous?

Marie Skłodowska-Curie:
• born 1867 (Poland) / died 1934
• went to Paris 1891
• met Pierre Curie 1892 / married 1895
• discovered radium together
• Marie first woman to use word 'radioactive'
• Pierre and Marie / Nobel Prize 1903 (Marie first ever woman)
• Pierre member 'Académie Française' 1904 (not Marie / woman)
• Pierre died / 1904 / accident

Marie Skłodowska-Curie was born in Poland in 1867. Her father used to be a Physics teacher, and she enjoyed Physics at school. Marie went to Paris in 1891, where she met a scientist called Pierre Curie in 1892. They got married in 1895.

Together, Pierre and Marie discovered radium – an element that is very important for nuclear science. Marie Skłodowska-Curie was the first person who used the word 'radioactive'.

In 1903, Marie became the first woman to win a Nobel Prize – she shared it with Pierre.

In 1904, Pierre became a member of the 'Académie Française'. Women weren't allowed to become members, so Marie was never accepted by them.

Pierre died in an accident in 1906, but Marie went on working until she died in 1934.

(b) Write a short article about someone famous in science or medicine. Choose one of these two people. Use the notes and Dave's article to help you.

Christiaan Barnard
born 1922 (South Africa) / died 2001 / became doctor 1953 specialised in the heart 1967: first heart transplant (heart from dead woman into 55 year old man – died 18 days later)
Second transplant 1968: man / lived 563 days

Alexander Fleming
born 1881 (Scotland) / died 1955 / became professor of medicine 1928 specialised in antiseptics
1928: discovered penicillin
1945: won Nobel Prize with two other scientists (Florey & Chain)

For your portfolio

14 If I had ...

* Second conditional
* Vocabulary: information technology and computers

1 Read and listen

a How often do you use a computer? What do you use it for? What do your friends or family use a computer for?

b Read the magazine article quickly and find out which teenager thinks computers are:

* good fun
* important for everything
* not as good as books

COMPUTERS
– good for learning, or just for fun?

**Most of us use computers now, but what for?
How would our lives be different, if we didn't have them?
We talked to three teenagers to find out.**

Jeremy: 15, Sunderland	Mandy: 15, Leeds	Adrian: 16, Birmingham

We've got computers at school, of course, and we have IT lessons – I enjoy learning how to use some of the software. There are some brilliant programs for drawing and designing. But I don't like games or chat rooms so I don't use the computer for fun. I hate looking for information on the Internet, it's really boring, and not as quick and easy as reading books. But we would need more books in our library, if we didn't have computers.

I don't have a computer at home, but if I had one, I'd only use it for emails.

I think computers are 100% important in our lives. We've got one at home, but everyone in my family uses it. If I had enough money, I'd buy a laptop of my own. I use the computer for all kinds of things – homework, projects, chat, emailing people, playing games, everything! If we didn't have one, I don't know what I would do! I suppose I'd write letters or phone my friends more, and I'd have to read books! But you can learn so much more on the net!

I think the Internet's amazing and that's how I use my computer most – I chat! If I had the time, I'd start my own website, but it would be a lot of work, and I probably wouldn't have time for that and school. If I had my own site, I'd put video shows, links to sports pages and chat rooms for other teenagers on it. I'm sure it would be loads of fun! Without computers, our lives would be really boring.

c  Read the article again and listen. Mark the sentences *T* (true) or *F* (false).

1 Jeremy thinks the Internet is fun. ☐
2 Jeremy has got a computer at home. ☐
3 Mandy is happy to share a computer with her family. ☐
4 Mandy thinks the Internet is better than books. ☐
5 Adrian hasn't started his own website. ☐
6 Adrian thinks computers make life interesting. ☐

2 Grammar

Second conditional

(a) Look at these sentences from the text. Are they about real or imagined situations?

*... but **if** I **had** one, I**'d** only **use** it for emails.
If I **had** the time, I**'d start** my own website.*

(b) Find more examples of the second conditional in the text on page 96 and <u>underline</u> them. Then complete the rule.

> **Rule:** If I **had** my own site … it **would be** fun.
> *If +* _____ *simple, +* _____ */ wouldn't*
> *(would not) + verb.*

Look

In speaking and in informal writing, we often use *'d* instead of *would*, and *wouldn't* instead of *would not*.
*If we were richer, we**'d** buy a bigger house.*

(c) (Circle) the correct words.

1 If I (had) / *would have* a lot of money, I *bought* / (would buy) a new bike.

2 They *would pass* / *passed* their exams if they *would work* / *worked* harder.

3 If we *would live* / *lived* nearer school, we *wouldn't have* / *had* to go on the bus.

4 Rick *came* / *would come* to your party if you *asked* / *would ask* him.

5 If she *was* / *would be* really ill, she *went* / *would go* to see a doctor.

6 We *gave* / *would give* you her address if we *knew* / *would know* it ourselves.

(d) Complete the sentences with the correct form of the verbs.

1 I think it *'d be* (be) a great party if the music *wasn't* (not be) so slow.

2 What _____ (you/do) if your dog _____ (run) away?

3 She _____ (talk) to you if you _____ (be) nicer to her.

4 He _____ (do) more housework if he _____ (have) more time.

5 If they _____ (not have) a lot of money, they _____ (not buy) nice clothes.

6 Who _____ (you/invite) if you _____ (win) a holiday for two?

3 Pronunciation

'd

🔊 Turn to page 121.

4 Speak

(a) We often use *If I were you, I'd ...* to give advice. Work with a partner. Look at the problems and take turns to give advice.

A: *I'm bored!*   B: *If I were you, I'd read a book.*

1 I haven't got any money.
2 My parents don't understand me.
3 My girlfriend/boyfriend's left me.
4 I've got a headache.
5 I feel sick.
6 I'm tired all the time.

(b) Put the verbs in the correct form to make questions in the second conditional. Then ask and answer the questions.

A: *Where would you go if you could visit any country in the world?*
B: *I'm not sure. Perhaps I'd go to Mexico.*

1 Where ____ you ____ (go) if you ____ (can) visit any country in the world?

2 Where ____ you ____ (live) if you ____ (have to) live in a different town?

3 What ____ you ____ (buy) if you ____ (win) 10,000 Euros in the lottery?

4 If you ____ (can) marry any famous person you ____ (want), who ____ you ____ (marry)?

5 If you ____ (can) meet a famous person, who ____ you ____ (meet)?

6 What ____ (do) if you ____ (be) invisible for a day?

7 If you (can) have one wish ,what _____ you _____(wish) for?

5 Read

(a) Who do you think the girl in the photo is? What do you think she has done? Read the magazine article to check your ideas.

(b) Answer the questions.

1. When did Ashley get her first computer?
2. Why did she start Goosehead.com?
3. How old was Ashley when her website became very successful?
4. What kind of information does her book contain?
5. What does she say about friends?

(c) What is the meaning of the underlined words from the text?

1. surfing the Internet (paragraph 1)
2. launched a website (paragraph 2)
3. 100,000 hits every day (paragraph 2)
4. rely on them (paragraph 4)
5. provide a little inspiration (paragraph 5)?

The GooseHead guide to life

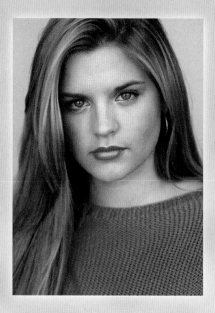

Ashley Power's mother bought a computer for her when she was eight. When she was thirteen, she was surfing the Internet regularly, but she couldn't find anywhere for teenagers to meet and talk. And one day she thought, 'If I had my own website, I'd make it a *really* interesting site for teenagers.'

So, when Ashley was sixteen, she launched her own website, called GooseHead. She had no idea how big a success it would be, but three years later, the site was the most successful teen site in the USA! It was getting 100,000 hits every day, and Ashley had about 30 employees.

After a few years, the website closed down. Then Ashley, who lives in Los Angeles, was asked to write a book called *The GooseHead Guide to Life*. The book is about how to design a website and start a business. It begins with a section called 'All About Ashley', where Ashley tells readers what it's like to be the boss of a company when you're only sixteen – not always easy! 'I was so happy. But it was crazy in a lot of ways. I got very stressed. I mean, I was only sixteen – I didn't even have a car! If you were sixteen and you had your own company, you'd be stressed, too!'

In her book, Ashley talks about the problems that teenagers have today, and about the importance of friendship, but also about being independent. 'Learn to love your friends but not rely on them. I did that by creating GooseHead on my own.'

Ashley says that *The GooseHead Guide to Life* is not a book of teenage advice. 'It isn't a book that's going to tell you what to do. I hope you can work that out for yourself,' she says. 'I just want to provide a little inspiration to teenagers. Maybe after reading my story, you'll launch your own website! But perhaps you've got a better idea? Well, if I were you, I'd just do it, whatever it is. Maybe it won't work – but maybe it will!'

From the #1 Teen Entertainment Network
GoOseHead.com

GoOseHead GuiDe to Life

Featuring:
GoOseLife
friends and crushes

Become a
GoOseWebMaSteR

Living in
GoOseWoRld

"Power created a site that made her more popular than any head cheerleader: The online teen hangout Goosehead.com attracts 100,000 visitors a day."
– People magazine

CEO of GoOseHead.com

6 Vocabulary

Information technology and computers

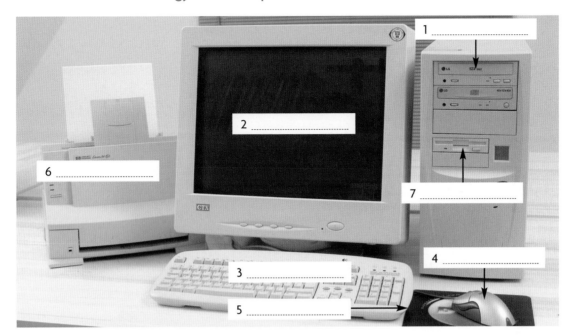

a 🔊 Match the words in the box with the numbered items in the pictures. Write the words in the spaces. Then listen, check and repeat.

> CD drive   disk drive
> keyboard   mouse
> mouse pad   printer
> screen

b 🔊 Complete the text with the correct form of the verbs in the box. Then listen and check.

> burn   crash   download
> log on   print   save
> search

When my grandmother was a little girl, the only person in her village with a telephone was the doctor, and Logie Baird was just inventing the television! But now she has a computer that she uses every day! She gets emails from all the family, so she [1] *starts up* her computer in the morning and [2] _____ to the Internet. She [3] _____ the net for information. She says it's better than walking to the library because it saves her old legs! She likes to [4] _____ all sorts of things for free, and then [5] _____ them out in full colour.

She gets angry if the computer [6] _____ and she has to start it up again. Once she lost some files so now she always [7] _____ everything on the hard disk. She even bought a CD writer the other day so now she can [8] _____ all her files on a CD.

The language of the Internet

c Match words 1–5 with definitions a–e.

1	online/offline	a	to put a page on the worldwide web
2	a chat room	b	software for finding web pages with the information you want
3	a provider	c	connected / not connected to the Internet
4	to publish (a page)	d	a place where you can 'talk' to other people online
5	a search engine	e	a company that gives you an Internet connection

7 Speak

Work with a partner. Ask and answer these questions.

- Which of the words on this page did you know already? How will you remember the new ones?

- Do you like surfing the Internet? Why / Why not?

- Do you always save the work you do on the computer? Have you ever lost anything?

Culture in mind

8 Read

(a) Work with a partner. Make a list of any problems you can have with computers.

(b) Now read the text. What problems with computers does the text mention? Tick (✓) the things on your list if you find them in the text.

JUST HOW GREAT *ARE* COMPUTERS?

Millions of people now use computers regularly for many different things – communication, study, entertainment and so on. We often hear that computers have changed our lives for the better. But have they?

Of course computers are great, and have changed some people's lives for the better. However, they can cause problems too. Many people who use computers a lot can get physical problems. They find that their eyesight gets worse, for example, if they look at the screen for too long. There can be injuries in computer users' hands and arms from making the same movements thousands of times, as people do with keyboards and a mouse. People who have computers are also spending more time sitting down, and less time exercising, so many of them are becoming overweight.

Other problems are psychological. One example is stress. Computers, the Internet and email have made many people's lives much faster. This can be very exciting, but it also means that people feel under a lot of pressure to do everything more quickly, which is stressful.

Addiction is also a problem with more and more young people. Many people have become addicted to using the Internet and chat rooms. They can spend hours and hours in chat rooms and surfing the net, sometimes until very late at night. This means they can't work or study properly and can have problems keeping friends.

Some studies in the United States have suggested that young children and teenagers who

spend many hours at computers can get lonely and even depressed.

'Computers can be a really positive part of children's lives. But parents and teachers need to help children learn to use computers in responsible and creative ways,' says teacher Jane Shields. 'And children need to learn when it is time to log off and do something different.'

c Answer the questions.

1 Describe the three types of physical problems mentioned in the text. How can they happen?

2 What psychological problems does the text mention? How can they happen?

3 What does Jane Shields think children need to learn to do?

9 Listen

a 🔊 Listen to three people talking about problems with computers. Match each speaker to a picture.

Speaker ....

Speaker ....

Speaker ....

b 🔊 Listen again and answer the questions.

1 How many hours a day does the first speaker spend on the computer?

2 How does he try to stop getting headaches?

3 What kind of work does the girl's father do?

4 What does her father wear?

5 What do the third speaker's friends think about him?

Discussion box

Work in pairs or small groups. Discuss these questions together.

1 What do you mostly use computers for?

2 Would you like to start your own website? Why / Why not?

3 What do you think computers will be like in five years?

4 What do you think your life would be like without computers?

10 Write

a Read the advertisement and Sam's article. Which topic did he choose to write about?

ABC Computers Competition!

Write a short article for our magazine (120–150 words) and you could win a new computer!

Write in English on <u>one</u> of these topics:

1 If you could study English on a computer or in a library, which would you choose?

2 Are computers important for you at home and at school? What would you do without them?

3 If you launched a website, what would it be like?

If I could study English on a computer or in a library, I would not choose the library!

I would have to be quiet in a library, and I would not find all the latest information. If another student had the book I wanted, I would have to wait. It would be boring.

If I studied on a computer, I would surf the Internet and find lots of websites in English. I could find a chat room and email other teenagers who speak English. There are CD-ROMs for learning languages and you can practise things you find difficult. You can record your own voice and then listen to it.

I would get all the information I needed if I worked on a computer — it would be really convenient.

b Write your entry to the competition and choose **one** of the other options, either 2 or 3. Use Sam's article to help you.

For your portfolio

15 Lost worlds

* Past perfect
* Vocabulary: noun suffixes -r, -er, -or and -ist

1 Read and listen

(a) Where is Machu Picchu? Who do you think lived there? Read the text quickly to find the answers.

(b) 🔊 Read the text again and listen. Answer the questions.

1 Where was Hiram Bingham on the morning of 24 July, 1911? Why?
2 How high up in the mountains was the hotel?
3 Who took Bingham to the wall?
4 What did Bingham see after he had climbed over the wall?

The discovery of Machu Picchu

The Incas

Between 1438 and 1532 the Incas built an empire with a population of about 12,000,000 people on the west coast of South America. They had no system of writing, so little is known about their everyday lives. But we *do* know these things:

* they built large cities in the mountains
* they built houses with huge square stones
* they built 23,000 kilometres of roads through the mountains
* they did not have wheels so everything was carried by animals or people

It was early morning on 24 July, 1911. A young American archaeologist named Hiram Bingham was in a small hotel in Peru, in the Andes mountains. He was there because he wanted to find a lost Inca city. He was not the first. Before Bingham, other explorers had looked for the city, but they hadn't found it.

Bingham had always been fascinated by the Incas. He was a university professor and had studied their civilisation for many years. Bingham and some scientists had travelled all the way to Peru from the USA, and had gone up to the city of Cuzco. From Cuzco, they had travelled higher up into the mountains, to about 1,800 metres, and they had spent the night in the hotel. The hotel owner had told Bingham about a 'lost' city not far away.

On the morning of 24 July, Bingham and a guide went out in the heavy tropical rain and climbed another 600 metres. On the way, they met a ten-year-old boy who led them through the jungle to a wall. They climbed over it and there it was: Machu Picchu – the lost city of the Incas!

In his book *'The discovery of Machu Picchu'* Hiram Bingham wrote: 'Suddenly I was standing in front of the walls of a ruin and houses from the best quality of Inca art … I found brilliant temples, royal houses, a big square and tens of houses. It looked like a dream.'

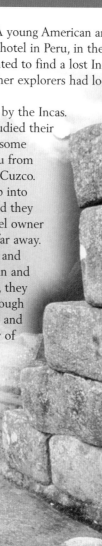

2 Grammar

Past perfect

a) Look at the information in the box. Then read sentences 1–5 and write A or B in the boxes.

> **A** = on the morning of 24 July, 1911 **B** = before the morning of 24 July, 1911

1   Other explorers **had looked** for the lost city, but they **hadn't found** it.
2   Bingham **had studied** the Inca civilisation for many years.
3   Professor Bingham and his friends **had travelled** from the USA.
4   They **met** a ten-year-old boy.
5   They **climbed** over the wall.
6   Professor Bingham **had waited** a long time for this moment.

b) In Exercise 2a, the verbs in 1, 2, 3 and 6 are in the past perfect. <u>Underline</u> other examples of the past perfect in the text on page 102. Then complete the rule and the table.

> **Rule:** (Circle) the correct word(s).
>
> Use the past perfect to make it clear that one action happened *before / at the same time as* another action in the past.

Positive	Negative	Question	Short answer
I/you/we/they/he/she/it/ **had** changed.	I/you/we/they/he/she/it _____ **(had not)** changed.	_____ I/you/we/they/he/she/it changed?	Yes, I/you/we/they/he/she/it _____ . No, I/you/we/they/he//she/it _____ **(had not)**.

c) Complete the sentences. Use the past perfect form of the verbs.

1   When I got home, my brother *had gone* (go) out.
2   She couldn't get into the house because she _____ (lose) her keys.
3   My teacher was happy because I _____ (not make) any mistakes in the test.
4   We didn't eat dinner last night because we _____ (not buy) any food.
5   I didn't recognise my cousin because he _____ (change) a lot since the last time I saw him.
6   They missed the train. When they got to the station, it _____ already _____ (leave).
7   When I phoned last night, _____ you already _____ (go) to bed?

d) (Circle) the correct words.

1   In 1531 Francisco Pizarro ᵃ (went) / had gone to Peru to look for gold. When he arrived in Peru, he found that the Incas ᵇ built / had built a huge empire. People ᶜ lived / had lived in Peru for centuries when the Incas started building their empire.

2   Thor Heyerdahl, from Norway, ᵃ was / had been a famous explorer in the 20th century. After Heyerdahl ᵇ built / had built his famous ship the Kon-Tiki, he sailed in it from Peru to Polynesia in 1947. The Kon-Tiki ᶜ sailed / had sailed for more than 8,000 kilometres when it reached Polynesia. In 1955–1956, Heyerdahl ᵈ went on / had been on another expedition, this time to Easter Island.

e) Complete the sentences. Use the past simple or past perfect form of the verbs.

1   My mum was angry because I *hadn't done* (not do) my work.
2   Yesterday I _____ (lose) my bus pass, so I _____ (have to) pay and then I _____ (leave) my schoolbag on the bus.
3   It was good to see Carol last week. I _____ (not see) her for ages.
4   Twenty years ago, someone _____ (find) another Inca city. A lot of tourists _____ (go) there immediately to see it.
5   He _____ (not enjoy) the film very much last night, because he _____ (see) it before.

3 Pronunciation

had and *'d*

🔊 Turn to page 121.

4 Speak

a Work with a partner. Make as many correct sentences as you can with the words in the table.

I was late because I'd missed the bus.

I		angry		I		missed the bus.
My parents	was	unhappy		you	'd	worked very hard.
My friend		late	because	we		passed the test.
We		tired		they		come home late.
You	were	surprised		he	hadn't	practised a lot.
The teacher		excited		she		done a lot of shopping.

A story: Mel saves a small boy

b Find these things in pictures a–f.

a ladder   a kitten   a window cleaner   a small boy crying   a garage roof

c Work with a partner. Put the pictures in order to make a story. Write 2–6 in the boxes.

d Tell the story. Start with picture number 4.

Mel was going home from work. She was walking down the street, and when she looked up, she saw a toddler who had climbed on to a garage roof.

e Now tell the story again, but this time start with picture number 3.

f Think of a situation that you were in, in the past. Say what it was and why it happened.

A: *Two months ago, I couldn't get into my house because I'd lost my keys!*

B: *Last Friday I was late for school because my watch had stopped.*

5 Listen

The army of Xi'an

a terracotta figure
of a soldier

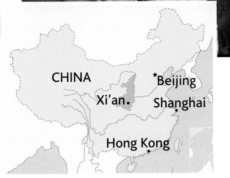

CHINA

*Beijing

Xi'an.   Shanghai

Hong Kong

(a) 🔊 Pictures a–f tell the story of how a terracotta army
was found in China. Put the pictures in order to make
the story. Write 1–6 in the boxes. Then listen to part of
a radio programme and check your answers.

a

b

c

d

1

e

f

(b) 🔊 Listen to the second part of the programme
and answer the questions.

1   How many terracotta figures were found?
2   In what ways are the figures different from each other?
3   Why were the figures made and put under the ground?
4   How long had the figures been under the ground?
5   How long did it take to make the figures?

6 Vocabulary

Noun suffixes -r, -er, -or
and -ist

(a) Find nouns in the text on page
102 that mean:

1   a person who works in
    archaeology *ar* _____
2   a person who explores other
    countries *ex* _____
3   a person who teaches at a
    university *pr* _____
4   people who work in science
    sc _____
5   a person who owns something
    o _____

(b) Use -r, -er, -ist or -or to make
nouns from the words.

1   decorate *decorator*   6   journal _____
2   art _____   7   farm _____
3   football _____   8   cycle _____
4   photograph _____   9   drive _____
5   tour _____   10 reception _____

(c) Complete the sentences.
Choose from the nouns
in Exercise 6b.

1   Picasso was a famous 20th
    century _____.
2   I love Aldo Sessa's photos of
    Argentina. I think he's the best
    _____ in the world!
3   The _____ is going to
    paint our living room next
    week.
4   When you leave the hotel,
    please remember to give your
    key to the _____ .
5   A dairy _____ has to get
    up early to milk the cows.
6   His dad's a _____ , he
    writes stories for the local
    newspaper.

I don't think so

7 Read and listen

(a) 🔊 Where are Dave and Amy? What do you think is going to happen? Read, listen and check your answers.

Dave: Are you sure you aren't coming back today, with me?

Amy: No, Dave. I told you – I'm talking to Saints Alive this afternoon.

Dave: Well, OK. Listen, Amy. I'm really sorry – I hadn't realised how upset you were about Joanne. I've been a bit stupid. All that stuff about you not being in the band any more.

Amy: It's OK, Dave. I think Joanne had already decided before the contest that she wanted my place in the band – and my boyfriend.

Dave: Oh, but ...

Amy: No really, it's OK. I mean, you didn't lie to me, did you? I asked you and you told me.

Dave: It *was* Joanne's idea, actually – but I don't know why I didn't say 'no' right away.

Amy: Well, I wasn't very happy about it.

Dave: No ... I know. Look, I don't think Joanne wants to stay in the band. Anyway, I don't want her to stay. I'm hoping that *you'll* stay, though.

Amy: I don't think so, Dave. We'd been together for quite a long time, hadn't we – before we started the band?

Dave: But Amy ...!

Amy: I know I'm not the world's greatest singer, Dave, but I *do* want to give it a go.

Dave: Yes, sure, Amy, I understand about the band. And good luck. You're great!

Amy: That's sweet, Dave, thanks.

Dave: And I hope that ... you know ... you and me, we can still ...

Amy: Same answer, Dave – I don't think so.

Dave: My bus is going to leave. I have to go.

Amy: Me too – I don't want to be late.

Dave: Amy, will you call me later tonight?

Amy: Well ... OK.

Dave: Good luck again. I'll see you, Amy.

Amy: ... maybe.

(b) Mark the sentences *T* (true), *F* (false) or *N* (not enough information).

1 Dave doesn't want Amy to go back to Cambridge with him. ☐
2 Dave apologises to Amy. ☐
3 Amy is still very angry with Dave. ☐
4 Dave wants both Amy and Matt to stay in the band. ☐
5 Amy thinks she's an excellent singer. ☐
6 Dave still wants to be Amy's boyfriend. ☐
7 Amy is going to call Dave later. ☐

8 Everyday English

a) Find expressions 1–4 in the story. Who says them? How do you say them in your language?

1 all that <u>stuff</u>
2 I'm hoping that you'll stay, <u>though</u>.
3 I want to <u>give it a go</u>.
4 <u>Good luck</u>.

b) Complete the sentences with the <u>underlined</u> words in Exercise 8a.

1 Luke: I'm playing in a squash competition tomorrow. I'm not really a very good player, but I'm going to _____ .
Ben: Really? Great, _____ !

2 Amelia: Do you like history?
Sam: Yes, I think it's really interesting. Famous people, important things that happened in the past, _____ like that – it's great!

3 Edward: Can you come round to my place at 8 o'clock?
Markus: Sorry, I'm busy till 8. I can come at 9.30, _____ .

9 Write

A short story

a) Read the story and match it to one of the pictures.

b) Match the topics with the paragraphs in the text. Write A–D in the boxes.

1 What the person found, and what it looked like. ☐
2 What happened in the end, and an explanation for the event. ☐
3 Setting the scene (where the person was, what the weather was like etc.). ☐
4 What the person did after finding the object. ☐

c) Look at the <u>underlined</u> words in the story. Which ones describe:

● the time that things happened?
● the order in which things happened?

Which of the <u>underlined</u> words are used to make the story more interesting?

d) Write a story about something you found. Choose one of the other pictures in Exercise 9a, or write your own story. Use the <u>underlined</u> expressions in the story.

A <u>About a month ago</u>, I was walking alone on the beach on a warm evening. I had finished all my homework, and I wanted to relax.

B <u>Suddenly</u>, I saw two small children who were digging in the sand. They had found something, and they were looking at it. It was big, reddish-brown and made of metal. <u>When</u> I looked at it, I knew <u>immediately</u> that it was an old bomb!

C <u>First</u>, I told the children to move away from the bomb. <u>Fortunately</u>, I had my mobile phone with me, so I called the police and told them what we had found. <u>Fifteen minutes later</u>, the police arrived and I explained everything to them. <u>Then</u> I went home again.

D <u>The next day</u>, I read in the newspaper that the police had blown the bomb up. It had been in the sand on the beach for over sixty years. It was from the Second World War, and it was very dangerous!

For your portfolio

16 Good or bad luck?

* Reported statements and questions
* Third conditional
* Vocabulary: noun suffixes, -ation and -ment

He was looking for the fathe
She was looking for a sec

CENT
STATIO

WINNER
GOLDEN BEAR
BERLIN FILM FESTIVAL 19
BEST PICTURE • BEST ACTRESS

A SONY PICTURES CLASSICS RELEASE An ARTHUR COHN Production "CENTRAL STATION"

www.sonyclassics.com

1 Read and listen

a There is a story that connects all of the pictures. What is it, do you think? Read the article to check your ideas.

A lucky break for the shoeshine boy

In 1998, twelve-year-old Vinícius de Oliveira from Rio de Janeiro in Brazil became a film star in the film *Central do Brasil*, or *Central Station* in English. The film got an Oscar nomination for Best Foreign Film.

But Vinícius was not always a star. Before he made the film, he was a shoeshine boy, cleaning people's shoes in the streets of Rio de Janeiro.

In 1997, Vinícius was just eleven years old, with almost no education. He worked at an airport in Rio de Janeiro, cleaning the shoes of businessmen. One day, he asked a man if he wanted him to clean his shoes, but the man said 'no', because he was wearing trainers!

Vinícius was poor, so he asked the man if he had any money, and a conversation started. First, the man asked him what his name was, then he asked Vinícius where he lived, how old he was, and so on. And then came the real surprise – he said he wanted Vinícius to do a film test! The man was the Brazilian film director, Walter Salles.

At first Vinícius said 'no'. He told Salles that he couldn't act, and that he'd never seen a film because he had no money for entertainment. But Salles continued talking to him, and Vinícius asked if the other shoeshine boys could also do the film test, so that they could have a chance too. Salles agreed, and Vinícius said he would do the test. But it was Vinícius who got the part.

After the test, Walter Salles asked him if he would take the part of Josué, the boy in the film. Vinícius had really enjoyed the test, so he agreed, and asked Salles when he could start.

Salles said he was very happy with Vinícius' performance in the film. Vinícius was not the first boy that Salles had asked – he'd tested 1,500 boys before he found him! So that day at the airport was very lucky for the shoeshine boy. If he hadn't been there that day, he would never have become a film star. And if Walter Salles hadn't been wearing trainers, perhaps he would never have started talking to Vinícius!

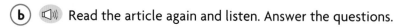

b Read the article again and listen. Answer the questions.

1 How old was Vinícius when Walter Salles met him?
2 Why did Salles not want Vinícius to clean his shoes?
3 Why did Vinícius ask the man to give him some money?
4 Why did Vinícius say 'no' when Salles first asked him to do a film test?
5 When did Vinícius say 'yes' to Salles?
6 How many tests had Salles done before he met Vinícius?
7 Why was that day at the airport 'a lucky break' for Vinícius?

2 Grammar

Reported statements

a Who said these things in the text on page 108? Write *Vinícius* or *Salles* on the lines.

1 'I want you to do a film test.'   *Salles*   *said* ....
2 'I can't act.'   ....   *told* ....
3 'I've never seen a film.'   ....   *said* ....
4 'I'll do the test.'   ....   *said* ....
5 'I'm very happy with his performance.' ....   *said* ....

b How are the statements above reported in the text on page 108? Find the reported statements in the text and complete the sentences in Exercise 2a.

c Look at the direct speech and reported statements in Exercise 2a. Complete the table.

Direct speech	→	Reported speech
Present simple	→	....
Past simple	→	Past perfect simple
Present perfect	→	....
am / is / are going to	→	*was / were going to*
can/can't	→	....
will/won't	→	....

d Put the reported speech into direct speech.

1 Vinícius said he was eleven years old.
   'I'm eleven years old,' said Vinícius.

2 The boy said he lived in Rio.
   'I .... ,'
   said the boy.

3 Salles said he was going to make a film.
   '..
   .... ,'
   said Salles.

4 Salles said the other boys could come.
   '..
   .... ,'
   said Salles.

5 He said Vinícius would earn a lot of money.
   '..
   .... ,'
   he said.

6 He said he hadn't seen a better young actor.
   '..
   .... ,'
   said Salles.

e Put the direct speech into reported speech.

1 'I'm tired,' said Tom.
   Tom said (that) he was tired.

2 'I'm going home,' he said.
   He said he .... home.

3 'I've worked hard,' said Maria.
   Maria said she .... hard.

4 'I'll do my homework later,' John told Kim.
   John told Kim he .... later.

5 'You can phone me, Laura,' I said.
   I told Laura she .... me.

6 'I've never had so much luck,' said Kim.
   Kim said she .... so much luck.

3 Vocabulary

Noun suffixes, *-ation* and *-ment*

Complete the sentences. Use the noun forms of the verbs.

1 Street children in Brazil need better   *education* . (educate)

2 My teacher says she's noticed a real .... in my French. (improve)

3 I think email is a much better form of .... than letters. (communicate)

4 Our school needs some new computer .... (equip)

5 Excuse me, could you give me some .... about buses please? (inform)

6 I did a quick .... to see how much money I'd spent. (calculate)

7 He studied hotel .... and now he's the manager of a hotel in Paris. (manage)

4 Grammar

Reported questions

a Match the direct questions 1–4 with the reported questions a–d.
Who asked each question, Vinícius or Salles?

1 'Do you want me to clean your shoes?'
2 'How old are you?'
3 'Have you got any money, please?'
4 'Where do you live?'

a He asked him where he lived.
b He asked him if he wanted him to clean his shoes.
c He asked him how old he was.
d He asked him if he had any money.

b Look at questions 1–4 in Exercise 4a. Which questions are *yes/no* questions?
Which ones use question words? Find other examples of reported questions in
the text on page 108 and underline them. Then look at the table and complete the rule.

He asked him		he had (got) any money.
Harry asked us	if	we were happy.
We asked them		they lived near us.
We asked them	where	they lived.
Tomas asked Klara	what	she was doing.
They asked us	when	we were going to the party.
He asked me	how	my mum was.

Rule:
- Never use the auxiliaries .... , ... or *did* in reported questions.
- When reporting open questions, the word order is the same as for statements.
- When reporting *yes/no* questions, use the word .... before the object and main verb.

c Put the words in the correct order to make sentences.

Marcus got home late one night. His parents asked him a lot of questions when he got home. At school, he told his friend Jordan about it.

1 if/asked/was/OK/they/me/I _They asked me if I was OK_ .
2 they/why/late/I/was/asked/me _____ .
3 asked/were/I/angry/if/them/they _I_____ .
4 they/me/where/I'd been/asked _They_____ .
5 asked/could/I/them/if/I/go out again/on Saturday
   _I_____ .
6 wanted/where/asked/I/they/me/to go _____ .

d 🔊 Joe's aunt from Australia visited him last week and she asked him a lot of questions! Listen to their conversation and write down her questions.

'_How old are you, Joe?_' _____

e Now write the questions in reported speech.

She asked him how old he was. _____

f 🔊 Listen to the conversation again and note Joe's answers. Then write Joe's answers in reported speech.

He said he'd be 16 next birthday. _____

5 Speak

Work with a partner. Student A: look at this page.
Student B: turn to page 123.

Student A: ask Student B these questions, but don't write the answers down; you must remember them! Then find another partner and tell him/her what you found out about Student B. You start.

I asked (Maria) if she could remember her first day at school. She said ...

- Can you remember your first day at school?
- What did you have for breakfast this morning?
- What did you do last Saturday?
- Have you been to the USA?

6 Listen

(a) 🔊 Jack phoned Sarah yesterday. Listen to their conversation and answer the questions.

1 Where did Jack invite Sarah to go?
2 What time did they arrange to meet?

(b) 🔊 Things didn't go well! Look at the pictures and see what happened. Try to put them in the correct order. Then listen to Jack's conversation with Daisy and check your answers.

Jack's unlucky day

(c) 🔊 Listen to their conversation again and complete the sentences with the correct verbs.

Daisy: I hear you missed your date with Sarah last night, Jack.

Jack: Yeah, it was terrible! If I'd _looked_ at my watch before, I'd have been OK.

Daisy: What do you mean?

Jack: Well, I left the house late and I ran. If I hadn't ¹_____, my glasses wouldn't have ²_____ .

Daisy: Your glasses?

Jack: Yeah, they fell off and broke on the ground. So I had to go home and get my other ones. Then I decided to catch the bus, but it was late! If the bus ³_____ arrived on time, I ⁴_____ have been late!

Daisy: And if you ⁵_____ been late, you'd have seen the film with Sarah!

(b) Underline other examples of the third conditional in Jack and Daisy's conversation in Exercise 6c.

(c) Complete the sentences. Use the correct form of the verbs.

1 If I _'d known_ (know) it was your birthday, I _would have bought_ (buy) you a present.

2 If you _____ (study) harder, you _____ (pass) your exams.

3 We _____ (not win) the game if we _____ (not play) well.

4 John _____ (buy) the new trainers if he _____ (have) enough money.

5 Jack _____ (go) to the cinema with Sarah if he _____ (look) at his watch earlier.

6 We _____ (not get wet) if we _____ (take) our umbrellas.

7 Grammar

Third conditional

(a) Look at the examples. Then complete the rule.

*If I'd **looked** at my watch before, I'd have been OK.*
*If I **hadn't run**, my glasses **wouldn't have fallen off**.*

> **Rule:** If I'd looked, I'd have been OK.
> If + _____ would(n't) _____ + past participle
>
> ● Use the third conditional to talk about imagined situations in the past.

8 Pronunciation

would ('d) have / wouldn't have

🔊 Turn to page 121.

Culture in mind

9 Read and listen

a 🔊 Numbers 1 to 6 are examples of some superstitions in Britain. In the boxes, write B (bad luck) if you think they mean bad luck, and a G (good luck) if you think they mean good luck. Then listen and check your answers.

1   a black cat
2   walking under a ladder
3   a horseshoe
4   a broken mirror
5   touching wood
6   opening an umbrella indoors

b Now read about how people think some superstitions started.

Witch

Where do SUPERSTITIONS come from?

It's actually very hard to know where, when and how superstitions started, but many of the superstitions in Britain are connected to the idea of evil spirits, witches and the devil. Take, for example, the idea of 'touching wood'. In ancient times in Britain, many people believed that evil spirits lived in trees, and that they could come down into the earth. But if someone touched the tree, then the spirit would not be able to come out – that's why people 'touch wood', to keep the evil spirits away.

Another 'good luck' superstition is the horseshoe. Perhaps this is because it is shaped like a new moon, and a new moon always used to be seen as something positive. But we don't really know!

Superstitions about black cats are more complicated. Some people believe they are good luck, and others believe they are bad luck. Black cats were usually a witch's pet – and witches were definitely bad luck! However, fishermen's wives sometimes used to keep a black cat at home to prevent an accident at sea, and so black cats were believed to be valuable and were often stolen.

Finally, there's a British superstition that if you spill salt, you should take a little of the salt and throw it over your left shoulder. This is because it was thought that the Devil is always waiting behind your left shoulder, so if you throw some salt there, it will go in his eye – and that will bring you good luck!

Evil

c Answer the questions.

1 Are we very sure of where superstitions come from?

2 What did people use to think lived in trees?

3 What did horseshoes remind people of?

4 Why did fishermen's wives use to keep a black cat at home?

5 Why do people sometimes throw salt over their left shoulder?

It

Devil

Discussion box

Work in pairs or small groups. Discuss these questions together.

1 Do you have any of these superstitions in your country? Do they mean the same things?

2 Do you know of any other superstitions in other countries?

3 Are you superstitious? If yes, give an example.

10 Write

a Jack (from page 111) wrote an email to Sarah. Read his email and find three more things which aren't true.

Example: *He said his watch had broken, but in fact he left the house late.*

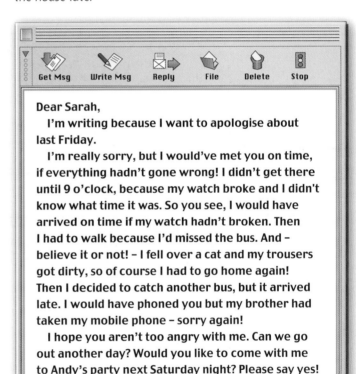

Get Msg   Write Msg   Reply   File   Delete   Stop

Dear Sarah,

I'm writing because I want to apologise about last Friday.

I'm really sorry, but I would've met you on time, if everything hadn't gone wrong! I didn't get there until 9 o'clock, because my watch broke and I didn't know what time it was. So you see, I would have arrived on time if my watch hadn't broken. Then I had to walk because I'd missed the bus. And – believe it or not! – I fell over a cat and my trousers got dirty, so of course I had to go home again! Then I decided to catch another bus, but it arrived late. I would have phoned you but my brother had taken my mobile phone – sorry again!

I hope you aren't too angry with me. Can we go out another day? Would you like to come with me to Andy's party next Saturday night? Please say yes!

Looking forward to hearing from you,

Jack

b Read the email again. What words does Jack use to:

1 apologise?   2 invite Sarah to the party?

c You arranged to go on a date with a friend. You agreed to meet at your favourite café at 6.30, but when you arrived at 7.30 your friend had already left. Why were you late? Think of some reasons (they must be different from Jack's!) and write them down.

d Write an email to your friend. Apologise for not meeting him/her, and tell him/her what happened. Use Jack's email to help you.

For your portfolio

Module 4 **Check your progress**

1 **Grammar**

a Complete the sentences with the correct relative pronouns: *who*, *that*, *where* or *which*. Sometimes there are two correct answers.

1 That's the boy _who/that_ scored three goals yesterday.
2 I love the shop _____ I bought this shirt.
3 I don't like people _____ don't laugh at my jokes!
4 Our neighbours have got a dog _____ always makes a lot of noise.
5 Last night I downloaded a computer program _____ lets you play music on the computer.
6 There's a girl in our class _____ speaks perfect Spanish. [ ] 5

b Complete the sentences. Use the present simple, or the correct form of *used to*.

1 That shop _used to sell_ (sell) CDs, but now it _'s_ (be) a supermarket.
2 My grandparents _____ (live) in France now, but they _____ (live) in London.
3 I _____ (enjoy) Maths a lot now, but when I was younger, I _____ (hate) it!
4 My sister _____ (eat) a lot of chips, but she _____ (not like) them any more.
5 I _____ (not use) my mobile phone very much, but now I _____ (use) it a lot!
6 A: _____ you _____ (have) bad dreams when _____ you were a child?
   B: Yes, I did, but I _____ (not have) them any more. [ ] 5

c Complete the sentences. Use the correct form of the verbs.

1 If I _had_ (have) enough money, I _'d buy_ (buy) a new computer.
2 If I _____ (know) her name, I _____ (tell) you.
3 _____ he _____ (surf) the net all day, if he _____ (have) a computer?
4 If we _____ (get) home after midnight, _____ your parents _____ (be) angry?
5 I'm sure he _____ (go) out with you, if you _____ (ask) him.
6 If there _____ (be) a good clothes shop in town, I _____ (not buy) my clothes here. [ ] 5

d Complete the sentences. Use the past simple or past perfect form of the verbs.

1 I _enjoyed_ (enjoy) the film a lot yesterday. I _hadn't watched_ (watch) a comedy for a long time.
2 I _____ (feel) really tired yesterday because I _____ (not sleep) well the night before.
3 We _____ (have) great fun last summer. We _____ (not be) to the sea since 2001.
4 The house _____ (be) really cold because someone _____ (forget) to close the windows before we left.
5 _____ John _____ (live) in London for a long time before he _____ (move) to Oxford?
6 _____ they _____ (know) each other for a long time before they _____ (get married)? [ ] 5

e Put the direct speech into reported speech.

1 'I'm bored,' she said. _She said she was bored._
2 'I want to go home,' said my little brother. _My little brother said_ _____
3 'I didn't do my homework,' he told the teacher. _He told the teacher_ _____
4 'I'll pay for the meal,' said Luis.
   _____
5 'Your brother can't come,' my aunt told me.
   _____
6 'I've never been to the USA,' he said.
   _____ [ ] 5

f Put the direct speech into reported speech.

1 'Are you tired?' Guy asked me. _Guy asked me if I was tired._
2 'Do you like this music?' she asked me. _She asked me_ _____
3 'Where do you live?' Jean asked Andy. _He asked her_ _____
4 'Did you buy that shirt in London?' Sally asked me.
   _____
5 'Where are you going?' I asked her.
   _____
6 'Have you ever been to Italy?' he asked me.
   _____ [ ] 5

8 (Circle) the correct words.

1 If we *didn't wake / hadn't woken* up late yesterday, we *weren't / wouldn't have been* late for school.

2 I *didn't buy / wouldn't have bought* it for you if I *knew / had known* you already had it.

3 If I *had known / would have known* the answer, I *had told / would have told* you.

4 We *had phoned / would've phoned* you if we *hadn't forgotten / wouldn't have forgotten* your number.

5 What *had you done / would you have done* if your parents *had found / would have found* out?

☐ 4

2 Vocabulary

a Complete the sentences with the words in the box.

> ambulance   pain   temperature
> tablet   hurt   ~~dentist~~   patient

1 I've got toothache so I'm going to see the *dentist* .

2 John was taken to hospital in an _____ .

3 I fell over and now I've got a _____ here.

4 Aspirin is a common _____ that's taken for headaches.

5 Jenny's got flu and a _____ of 40°.

6 I've been walking all day, and my legs really _____ now!

7 I'm Doctor Chen's new _____ .

☐ 6

b Write the words from the box in the lists.

> ~~keyboard~~   disk drive   ~~print~~   mouse
> ~~search~~   log on   CD drive   start up
> offline   crash   burn   chat room

Parts of a computer	The Internet	Using a computer
keyboard	*search*	*print*
_____	_____	_____
_____	_____	_____
_____	_____	_____

☐ 9

c Complete the sentences. Use the correct form of the words.

1 Those people are on holiday here – they're *tourists* . (tour)

2 My father's the _____ of that shop. (own)

3 Einstein was a famous _____ . (science)

4 Well done, James, you've made a lot of _____ to your composition. (improve)

5 We need new sports _____ . (equip)

6 There's lots of useful _____ . (inform)

7 My sister's a _____ at the new hotel. (reception)

☐ 6

3 Everyday English

Complete the dialogue with the words in the box.

> you're kidding   ~~congratulations~~
> end up with   stuff   though   give it a go

Ben: Hey Anna, ¹ *congratulations* ! I hear you've won a prize for designing a web page.

Anna: Thanks, Ben. It wasn't only me, ² _____ . Steve, Angela and Harry worked on it with me.

Ben: Harry? ³ _____ ! He doesn't know anything about computers!

Anna: Well, he does now! He decided to ⁴ _____ , and he learned how to do it. Now he's on the computer all day downloading games and ⁵ _____ like that.

Ben: Really? Well, he needs to be careful, or he'll ⁶ _____ bad eyesight, like my dad.

Anna: No, I don't think so, Ben!

☐ 5

How did you do?

Tick (✓) a box for each section.

Total score	😊	😐	🙁
☐ **60**	Very good	OK	Not very good
Grammar	26 – 34	20 – 25	less than 20
Vocabulary	17 – 21	12 – 16	less than 12
Everyday English	4 – 5	3	less than 3

Project 1

A group presentation

1 Do your research

a Work in groups of three or four. In your group, decide what you think is the best and most useful invention in the world. Choose an invention from the pictures, or your own idea.

The car

Glasses

The computer

The personal stereo

The wheel

The plane

The mobile phone

The Internet

b Make a list of reasons why you think the invention is so important. Look at Mark's example below. He chose the mobile phone.

- The mobile phone is a quick and easy way to communicate with other people.
- You can phone someone wherever you are.
- Before mobile phones, people had to use public pay phones. These often break and you need the right money!
- Mobile phones are very flexible: you can use them to send text messages and photos, as well as talk to someone.
- Mobile phones are more personal than email because you can hear the person you are talking to.
- Unlike some other inventions, the mobile phone does not damage the environment very much.

c Do some research to find out more about the invention you have chosen. For example, when was it invented and who invented it? Use an encyclopaedia or the Internet to help you. Get some pictures to illustrate your presentation.

2 Prepare the presentation

a In your group, put all your information together and plan your presentation. Your presentation will need to be a minimum of two minutes. Use this plan to help you.

- What the invention is.
- Background information about the invention.
- Why you think it's useful.
- Why it's better than some other inventions.

b Decide who is going to talk and what each person will talk about. Everyone in the group should say something.

c Rehearse your presentation. Decide how and when you are going to use the pictures you have collected. Ask your teacher to help you with difficult language/pronunciation.

d Groups take turns to make their presentation.

Project 2

A class survey: how we have fun

1 Do the survey

a Work in groups of three or four. In your group, think of six questions that you can ask other students about how they have fun. Use question words like: *How often? When? What? Where? How long?* For example:

How often do you go out in the evening?
What's your favourite activity?

b Make a questionnaire with your questions, like this:

Survey: how we have fun

1 How often do you go out in the evening?

   a never ☐

   b once a week ☐

   c twice a week ☐

   d more than twice a week ☐

2 What's your favourite activity?

   a going to the cinema ☐

   b playing team sports ☐

   c listening to music ☐

   d watching TV ☐

   e something else (say what) ....

3 What do you do when you feel unhappy?

....

c Use your questionnaire. Ask as many other students in your class as you can, and make a note of their names and answers.

2 Write up the results

a Go back to your group and put all your answers together.

b Write sentences about your answers. Use headings or questions to organise your report. For example:

How often do we go out?

Everyone in the class goes out once a week or more. Less than half the class go out twice a week. Three people usually go out more than three times a week and one person only goes out once a week. Boys go out more often than girls ...

What are our favourite activities?

Most people enjoy playing team sports, and most people play sports more than once a week. Football is a bit more popular with boys than girls, but girls enjoy volleyball more than boys. Girls prefer shopping with their friends to ...

Project 3

A poster: homes around the world

1 Do your research

(a) Work in groups of three or four. Think about the different kinds of houses in your country. Then think about houses in different parts of the world. How different or similar are the houses? Talk about the kinds of people who live there. For example, the Inuits in Canada, Hollywood film stars in Beverley Hills, people who live in cities in China, etc.

(b) Research more information about the kinds of homes in the countries and places you talked about. For example: Where are they? What do they look like? What are they made of? What kinds of people usually live in them?

(c) In your group, choose <u>four</u> or <u>five</u> different kinds of homes. You could decide to choose them because they are all very different from each other, or because you think they are the most interesting.

2 Make the poster

(a) Find some pictures of the different homes you have chosen for your poster. If you can't find any pictures, draw some!

(b) Use the information you found in Exercise 1b to write short texts about each of the homes.

(c) At the top of a large piece of paper, write the title of your presentation. For example, *'Homes Around the World'*. Arrange your pictures and short texts on the poster paper. Leave space at the bottom.

(d) At the bottom of the paper, write a longer text. Write your group's opinions about the homes you have described.
For example:

> We think that the most interesting homes are the tents in Tibet because they are very different from homes in our country. We like the homes in ＿＿＿ because ＿＿＿ .

(e) Present your poster to the class. Be prepared to answer questions about it.

Project 4
Designing a website

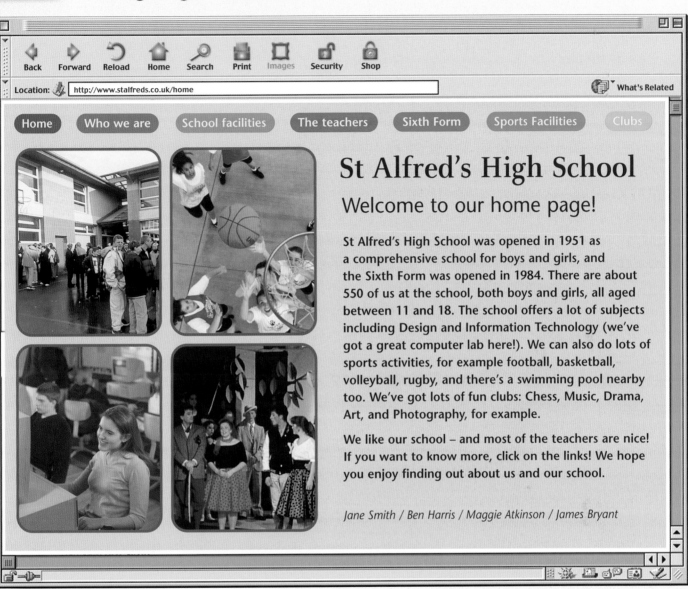

Back | **Forward** | **Reload** | **Home** | **Search** | **Print** | Images | **Security** | **Shop**

Location: http://www.stalfreds.co.uk/home   What's Related

Home | Who we are | School facilities | The teachers | Sixth Form | Sports Facilities | Clubs

St Alfred's High School
Welcome to our home page!

St Alfred's High School was opened in 1951 as a comprehensive school for boys and girls, and the Sixth Form was opened in 1984. There are about 550 of us at the school, both boys and girls, all aged between 11 and 18. The school offers a lot of subjects including Design and Information Technology (we've got a great computer lab here!). We can also do lots of sports activities, for example football, basketball, volleyball, rugby, and there's a swimming pool nearby too. We've got lots of fun clubs: Chess, Music, Drama, Art, and Photography, for example.

We like our school – and most of the teachers are nice! If you want to know more, click on the links! We hope you enjoy finding out about us and our school.

Jane Smith / Ben Harris / Maggie Atkinson / James Bryant

1 Prepare your website

(a) Work in groups of three or four. A school in Britain or the USA has asked you to design an English language web page of your school. Look at the web page about St Alfred's school. Who wrote it? What kind of information does it give?

(b) Think about your school. What kind of information do you want to write on the home page? Make notes.

(c) Look again at the web page for St Alfred's school. What kinds of links are there? What information and photos do you think there are in each link? Decide what links you want to have for your web page. Make a list and write notes for each page.

(d) Decide what pictures you will have on your website and how you will organise the texts, pictures and links.

2 Make your website

(a) Write your home page on a large piece of paper. Put your pictures where you want them on the page. Then do the same for your link pages.

(b) When all the groups have finished, put your web pages somewhere where everyone can see them. Compare what different groups have done.

For your portfolio

Pronunciation exercises

Unit 1

Linking sounds in the past simple

a 🔊 Listen to the sentences. How do you pronounce the <u>underlined</u> parts?

1 It happened <u>in</u> 1850.
2 Many people died <u>on</u> the way.
3 They wanted <u>a</u> lot of people.
4 It happened <u>last</u> night.
5 He died <u>ten</u> years ago.
6 We wanted <u>to</u> go home.

b 🔊 Listen again and repeat.

Unit 2

was and *were*

a 🔊 Listen to the sentences. Circle the examples of *was/wasn't* where it is weak. <u>Underline</u> the examples of *was/wasn't* where it is stressed.

1 What was he doing?
2 He was making a phone call.
3 He wasn't watching TV.
4 Was it raining?
5 Yes, it was.

b 🔊 Listen again and repeat.

c 🔊 Listen to these sentences. Circle the examples of *were/weren't* where it is weak. <u>Underline</u> the examples of *were/weren't* where it is stressed.

1 What were they doing?
2 They were sitting down.
3 They weren't having dinner.
4 Were they listening to music?
5 No, they weren't.

d 🔊 Listen again and repeat.

Unit 3

than and *as*

a 🔊 Listen and <u>underline</u> the stressed syllables.

1 Sarah's <u>bro</u>ther <u>isn't</u> as <u>old</u> as <u>she</u> is.
2 Peter's messier than his sister.
3 Peter isn't as tidy as his sister.
4 Travelling by train is often faster than travelling by bus.
5 Travelling by train isn't as slow as travelling by bus.

b 🔊 How do you pronounce *as* and *than*? Listen again, check and repeat.

Unit 4

/əʊ/ (w<u>on</u>'t)

🔊 Listen and repeat.

1 I won't open it.
2 He won't answer the question.
3 She won't tell me.
4 They won't come.
5 We won't be late.

Unit 5

Intonation in question tags

Your voice goes up ↑ in the tag if you aren't sure of the answer. It goes down ↓ if you think you know the answer, but you want to make conversation.

a 🔊 Listen to the sentences. Does the voice go up, or down at the end? Write *U* (up) or *D* (down).

1 You're from Canada, aren't you?
2 New York's the capital, isn't it?
3 You don't know much about Canada, do you?
4 There are 50 states, aren't there?
5 The USA's got a higher population than Canada, hasn't it?
6 People like ice hockey there, don't they?

b 🔊 Listen again and repeat.

Unit 6

/aʊ/ (all<u>ow</u>ed)

a 🔊 Listen and repeat.

1 now   2 how   3 out   4 shout
5 loud   6 allowed

b 🔊 <u>U</u>nderline the syllables with the /aʊ/ sound. Then listen, check and repeat.

1 How are you now?
2 I'm allowed to go out.
3 We're allowed to play loud music.
4 You aren't allowed to shout.

Unit 7

have, *has* and *for*

a 🔊 Listen and <u>underline</u> the stressed syllables.

1 How <u>long</u> have you been a <u>clown</u> <u>doc</u>tor?
2 For three years.
3 How long has she worked in London?
4 For a year.

b 🔊 How do you pronounce *have* and *has*? How do you pronounce *for*? Listen again and repeat.

Unit 8

Consonant clusters

a 🔊 Listen to the words. How do you pronounce the <u>underlined</u> letters? Listen again and repeat.

1 <u>sp</u>ace <u>tr</u>avel   2 <u>sc</u>ience fi<u>ct</u>ion
3 <u>scr</u>ipt   4 <u>dr</u>ama   5 <u>st</u>un<u>tw</u>oman
6 <u>fr</u>ightening   7 <u>thr</u>iller

b 🔊 Listen and repeat.

1 Alex does frightening stunts in thrillers.
2 Stuntwomen don't learn scripts.
3 I like science fiction films about space travel.

Unit 9

'Silent' letters

a 🔊 In many English words there are 'silent' letters which aren't pronounced. <u>Underline</u> the 'silent' letter(s) in each word. Then listen, check and repeat.

1 lis<u>t</u>en   2 bomb   3 write
4 build   5 knocked

b 🔊 Look at these words. <u>Underline</u> the 'silent' letter(s) in each example. Then listen, check and repeat.

1 answer   2 wrong   3 climb
4 high   5 mountain

c 🔊 Say the sentences. Then listen, check and repeat.

1 Listen and write.
2 It's the wrong answer.
3 He climbed a high mountain.
4 They're building a big bomb.

Unit 10

Sound and spelling: -ough

a 🔊 Listen and repeat.

1 enough   2 cough
3 through   4 tough

b 🔊 Say the sentences. Then listen, check and repeat.

1 I walked through the park.
2 I've got a very bad cough.
3 I can't eat this meat, it's too tough.
4 There aren't enough chairs.

Unit 11

must

a 🔊 Listen to the sentences. Circle the examples of must where it is weak. <u>Underline</u> the examples of must where it is stressed.

1 I (must) go now, it's late.
2 You must see that film, it's great!
3 You must remember to do your homework!
4 I must phone my friend tonight.
5 I must start doing some exercise!

b 🔊 Which sentences put a strong stress on must? Why, do you think? What happens to the t in the sentences where must is weak? Listen again and repeat.

Unit 12

Sentence stress: rhythm

a 🔊 <u>Underline</u> the syllables you think are stressed. Then listen and check.

1 Her <u>fa</u>ther's been <u>tea</u>ching <u>mu</u>sic for <u>ma</u>ny <u>years</u>.
2 The phone's been ringing all week.
3 She's been doing well at school.
4 How long has she been playing the violin?

b 🔊 Listen again and repeat.

Unit 13

/z/ or /s/ in used

a 🔊 Listen to the sentences. Circle the examples of used where it has a /z/ sound. <u>Underline</u> the examples of used where it has a /s/ sound.

1 I used the dictionary.
2 I used to watch a lot of videos.
3 Who used the computer?
4 John used to live in London.

Listen to the sentences again. Do you hear the 'd' in the word used?

b 🔊 Listen, check and repeat.

Unit 14

'd

a 🔊 Listen and circle the words you hear.

1 I read / I'd read a book.
2 I go / I'd go for a walk.
3 I close / I'd close the window.
4 I talk / I'd talk to the teacher.

b 🔊 Listen and repeat.

1 I'd go to the doctor.
2 I'd study more.
3 I'd search the Internet.
4 I'd go to the library.

Unit 15

had and 'd

a 🔊 Listen to the sentences. Circle the examples of had where it is weak. <u>Underline</u> the examples of had or hadn't where it is stressed.

1 I had a strange dream last night.
2 It was like a dream that had come true.
3 He had no time to help me.
4 Other explorers had looked for the city, but they hadn't found it.

b 🔊 Which sentences put a stronger stress on had? Why, do you think? Listen, check and repeat.

c 🔊 Listen and repeat.

1 There was no chocolate left. I'd eaten it all!
2 When the test finished, she'd only answered three questions!
3 We didn't go to the cinema because we'd seen the film before.
4 He didn't laugh at the joke because he'd heard it before.

Unit 16

would ('d) have / wouldn't have

a 🔊 Listen to the sentences. How do you pronounce the <u>underlined</u> parts?

1 <u>I'd have</u> been OK.
2 My glasses <u>wouldn't have</u> broken.
3 <u>I wouldn't have</u> been late.
4 You<u>'d have seen</u> the film.

b 🔊 Listen again and repeat.

Speaking exercises: extra material

Unit 1, page 7, Exercise 4

Student B: read the information about Kevin Hayes. Ask and answer questions to complete your missing information. Student A starts.

KEVIN HAYES is 28 years old. He lives in New York. Kevin loves .... , and he has a dangerous hobby; he climbs waterfalls! How is this possible? The answer is easy. He doesn't climb in summer, but he climbs in winter, when everything is frozen. At the moment, Kevin is .... He is planning a trip to the Canadian Rockies next January. He wants to .... there.

Kevin has to be very fit for his hobby, and he is doing a lot of exercise this month. Every day, he runs for an hour, and he goes to the gym. Many people think Kevin is .... 'Maybe I am,' he says. 'But I just love it!'

Unit 7, page 48, Exercise 4b

Are you fun to be with?

Less than 14 points
Your friends probably think you're quite serious and not usually great fun to be with. Life isn't so terrible you know! Sometimes it's good to have fun.

14 – 24 points
You're often fun to be with, but you can also be serious. Your friends know they can usually have a laugh with you, but when you're sad or angry you tell them.

25 – 36 points
You're always great fun to be with and people usually like you because they know they can have a good laugh with you. But you don't have to be fun *all* the time – perhaps sometimes you should be more serious!

Unit 9, page 63, Exercise 4a

Student B: Look at your information. Ask and answer the questions. Student A starts.

Student B

1 Where / London Bridge / move to in 1971? Alaska or Arizona?
   Where was London Bridge moved to in 1971?
2 When / the first television picture / produce? 1925 or 1950?
3 Which Beatle / the song *Imagine* / sing by? Paul McCartney or John Lennon?
4 Who / trainers / first invent by? Adidas or Nike?
5 When / Princess Diana / kill in a car crash? 1987 or 1997?

Unit 11, page 74, Exercise 1a

Look at the picture for 30 seconds. Then close your book and write down the things that you saw in the picture.

Unit 12, page 82, Exercise 5b

Student B: look at your information about David Bowie. Ask and answer questions to complete your missing information. Student A starts.

David Bowie

- He / sing / more than 30 years.
- He / play saxophone / .... years. (How long ...?)
- He / make records / more than 25 years.
- He / make / .... films. (How many ...?)
- He / marry to Iman / more than ten years.

Unit 13, page 93, Exercise 6a

(a) Think about when you were five or six years old. Read each question and tick (✓) the box if it is true for you. Put a cross (✗) if it is not true.

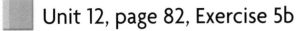

When you were small, did you use to ...?

		YOU	YOUR FRIEND
1	... go to bed after 9pm at weekends?	☐	☐
2	... have posters on your bedroom wall?	☐	☐
3	... have lots of friends?	☐	☐
4	... hate having a bath?	☐	☐
5	... worry about the clothes you wore?	☐	☐
6	... cry if you fell over?	☐	☐

(b) Now ask Student A about him/her, for example:

When I was small, I didn't use to go to bed after 9pm at weekends. Did you?

Put a tick (✓) or a cross (✗) in the boxes under 'your friend'.

Unit 16, page 110, Exercise 5

Student B

Ask Student A these questions, but don't write the answers down; you must remember them! Then find another partner and tell him/her what you found out about Student A. Student A starts.

I asked (Janek) if he could remember his first school exam. He said ...

- Can you remember your first school exam?
- What did you eat for dinner last night?
- What did you do last summer holidays?
- Have you been to England?

Irregular verbs and phonetics

Irregular verbs

Base form	Past simple	Past participle
be	was/were	been
beat	beat	beaten
become	became	become
begin	began	begun
blow	blew	blown
break	broke	broken
bring	brought	brought
build	built	built
buy	bought	bought
can	could	been able
catch	caught	caught
choose	chose	chosen
come	came	come
cost	cost	cost
cut	cut	cut
do	did	done
drink	drank	drunk
drive	drove	driven
eat	ate	eaten
fall	fell	fallen
feel	felt	felt
fight	fought	fought
find	found	found
fly	flew	flown
forget	forgot	forgotten
get	got	got
give	gave	given
go	went	gone
grow	grew	grown
have	had	had
hear	heard	heard
hit	hit	hit
hold	held	held
hurt	hurt	hurt
keep	kept	kept
know	knew	known
leave	left	left
let	let	let
lose	lost	lost
make	made	made
meet	met	met
pay	paid	paid
put	put	put
read	read	read
ride	rode	ridden
ring	rang	rung
run	ran	run
say	said	said
see	saw	seen
sell	sold	sold
send	sent	sent
shut	shut	shut
sing	sang	sung
sink	sank	sunk
sit	sat	sat
sleep	slept	slept
speak	spoke	spoken

Base form	Past simple	Past participle
spend	spent	spent
stand	stood	stood
steal	stole	stolen
swim	swam	swum
take	took	taken
teach	taught	taught
tell	told	told
think	thought	thought
understand	understood	understood
wake	woke	woken
wear	wore	worn
win	won	won
write	wrote	written

Phonetic symbols

Consonants

/p/	pen
/b/	be
/t/	two
/d/	do
/k/	can
/g/	good
/f/	five
/v/	very
/m/	make
/n/	nice
/ŋ/	sing
/s/	see
/z/	trousers
/w/	we
/l/	listen
/r/	right
/j/	you
/h/	he
/θ/	thing
/ð/	this
/ʃ/	she
/tʃ/	cheese
/ʒ/	usually
/dʒ/	German

Vowels

/æ/	man
/ɑː/	father
/e/	ten
/ɜː/	thirteen
/ə/	mother
/ɪ/	sit
/iː/	see
/ʊ/	book
/uː/	food
/ʌ/	up
/ɒ/	hot
/ɔː/	four

Diphthongs

/eɪ/	great
/aɪ/	fine
/ɔɪ/	boy
/ɪə/	hear
/eə/	chair
/aʊ/	town
/əʊ/	go
/ʊə/	pure

Wordlist

Unit 1

Verbs

attack /ə'tæk/
carry /'kæri/
catch /kætʃ/
climb /klaɪm/
control /kən'trəʊl/
die /daɪ/
emigrate /'emɪgreɪt/
explore /ɪk'splɔːr/
hope /həʊp/
imagine /ɪ'mædʒɪn/
send /send/
sink /sɪŋk/
try /traɪ/
win /wɪn/

Nouns

accident /'æksɪdənt/
bottom /'bɒtəm/
century /'senʃəri/
cholera /'kɒlərə/
competition /ˌkɒmpə'tɪʃən/
coral /'kɒrəl/
disease /dɪ'ziːz/
farmland /'fɑːmlænd/
gunshot /'gʌnʃɒt/
habitation /ˌhæbɪ'teɪʃən/
illness /'ɪlnəs/
journey /'dʒɜːni/
life /laɪf/
mountain /'maʊntɪn/
museum /mjuː'ziːəm/
Native American /ˌneɪtɪv
    ə'merɪkən/
ocean /'əʊʃən/
recording contract
    /rɪ'kɔːdɪŋ ˌkɒntrækt/
remains /rɪ'meɪnz/
settlement /'setlmənt/
settler /'setlər/
ship /ʃɪp/
shipwreck /'ʃɪprek/
site /'saɪt/
submarine /ˌsʌbmər'iːn/
trail /treɪl/
wagon /'wægən/
waterfall /'wɔːtəfɔːl/
wheel /'wɪːl/

Adjectives

accidental /ˌæksɪ'dentəl/
ancient /'eɪnʃənt/
barefoot /beə'fʊt/
brilliant /'brɪliənt/
dangerous /'deɪndʒərəs/
fit /fɪt/

frozen /'frəʊzən/
helpful /'helpfəl/
live /laɪv/
underwater /ˌʌndə'wɔːtər/

Everyday English

Actually /'æktʃʊəli/
bloke /bləʊk/
round here /'raʊnd 'hɪər/
Too right! /'tuː 'raɪt/

Unit 2

Fashion

baggy (adj) /'bægi/
beads (n) /biːdz/
button (n) /'bʌtən/
casual (adj) /'kæʒjuəl/
decorated (adj) /'dekəreɪtɪd/
denim (n, adj) /'denɪm/
dye (v, n) /daɪ/
fabric (n) /'fæbrɪk/
fashionable (adj) /'fæʃənəbl/
flared (adj) /fleərd/
low-waisted (adj)
    /ˌləʊ'weɪstɪd/
pattern (n) /'pætən/
straight (adj) /streɪt/
style (n) /staɪl/
trainers (n) /'treɪnərz/
trousers (n) /'traʊzəz/
wig (n) /wɪg/

Expressions with get

get angry /get 'æŋgri/
get an idea /get ən aɪ'dɪə/
get a surprise /get ə
    sə'praɪz/
get close /get 'kləʊs/
get home /get 'həʊm/
get old /get 'əʊld/
get the answer /get ðiː
    'ɑːnsər/
get to school /get tə 'skuːl/
get wet /get 'wet/

Verbs

go for a walk
    /ˌgəʊ fərə 'wɔːk/
invent /ɪn'vent/
laugh /lɑːf/
receive /rɪ'siːv/
stick /stɪk/

Nouns

binoculars /bɪ'nɒkjələz/
biro /'baɪrəʊ/
cave /keɪv/

concert /'kɒnsət/
cook /kʊk/
ink /ɪŋk/
invention /ɪn'venʃən/
inventor /ɪn'ventər/
stage /steɪdʒ/
surprise /sə'praɪz/
traffic light /'træfɪk laɪt/
typewriter /'taɪpˌraɪtər/
velcro /'velkrəʊ/

Adjectives

angry /'æŋgri/
informal /ɪn'fɔːməl/
popular /'pɒpjələr/
strong /strɒŋ/
tough /tʌf/

Adverbs

suddenly /'sʌdənli/

Unit 3

Sport

athlete (n) /'æθliːt/
break a record (v)
    /breɪk ə 'rekɔːd/
event (n) /ɪ'vent/
free diving (n) /'friː daɪvɪŋ/
gold medal (n)
    /gəʊld 'medəl/
gymnastics (n)
    /dʒɪm'næstɪks/
high jump (n) /'haɪ dʒʌmp/
jump (v, n) /dʒʌmp/
long jump (n) /'lɒŋ dʒʌmp/
practise (v) /'præktɪs/
score a goal (v) /skɔːr ə 'gəʊl/
snowboarding (n)
    /'snəʊbɔːdɪŋ/

Nouns

drummer /'drʌmər/
keyboards /'kiːbɔːdz/

Adjectives

confident /'kɒnfɪdənt/
deep /diːp/
dramatic /drə'mætɪk/
early /'ɜːli/
excellent /'eksələnt/
exciting /ɪk'saɪtɪŋ/
expensive /ɪk'spensɪv/
far /fɑːr/
fast /fɑːst/
fluent /'fluːənt/
hard /hɑːrd/
important /ɪm'pɔːtənt/

intelligent /ɪn'telɪdʒənt/
interesting /'ɪntrəstɪŋ/
low /ləʊ/
messy /'mesi/
nervous /'nɜːvəs/
noisy /'nɔɪzi/
pretty /'prɪti/
quiet /'kwaɪət/
shallow /'ʃæləʊ/
slim /slɪm/
successful /sək'sesfəl/
tidy /'taɪdi/
unsuccessful /ˌʌnsək'sesfəl/
useful /'juːsfəl/

Adverbs

badly /'bædli/
brilliantly /'brɪliəntli/
easily /'iːzəli/
fluently /'fluːəntli/
happily /'hæpɪli/
nervously /'nɜːvəsli/
quickly /'kwɪkli/
soon /suːn/
terribly /'terəbli/
well /wel/

Everyday English

have a go at (someone)
    /hæv ə 'gəʊ ət/
Hold on! /'həʊld 'ɒn/
I'm off! /aɪm 'ɒf/
Stop it! /'stɒp ɪt/

Unit 4

The environment / weather

atmosphere (n) /'ætməsfɪər/
climate change (n)
    /'klaɪmət tʃeɪndʒ/
coal (n) /kəʊl/
coastal (adj) /'kəʊstəl/
cycle lane (n) /'saɪkl ˌleɪn/
drop litter (v) /drɒp 'lɪtər/
litter (n) /'lɪtər/
energy source (n)
    /'enədʒi ˌsɔːs/
environment (n)
    /ɪn'vaɪərənmənt/
flood (v, n) /flʌd/
fragile (adj) /'frædʒaɪl/
fumes (n) /fjuːmz/
global warming (n)
    /ˌgləʊbəl 'wɔːmɪŋ/
hurricane (n) /'hʌrɪkən/

hydro-electric dam (n)
/ˌhaɪdrəʊɪlektrɪk 'dæm/
nuclear energy (n)
/ˌnjuːkliə^r 'enədʒi/
oil (n) /ɔɪl/
planet (n) /'plænɪt/
pole (n) /pəʊl/
pollute (v) /pə'luːt/
pollution (n) /pə'luːʃ^ən/
power station (n) /'paʊə^r
ˌsteɪʃ^ən/
rainforest (n) /'reɪnˌfɒrɪst/
recycle (v) /riː'saɪkl/
recycling (n) /riː'saɪklɪŋ/
renewable (adj) /rɪ'njuːəbl/
rubbish (n) /'rʌbɪʃ/
sea level (n) /'siː ˌlev^əl/
solar energy (n) /ˌsəʊlə^r
'enədʒi/
temperature change (n)
/'temprətʃə^r ˌtʃeɪndʒ/
thunderstorm (n)
/'θʌndəstɔːm/
tornado (n) /tɔː'neɪdəʊ/
traffic (n) /'træfɪk/
twister (n) /'twɪstə^r/
wave (n) /weɪv/
whirlwind (n) /'wɜːlwɪnd/
wind energy (n)
/'wɪnd ˌenədʒi/

Verbs

breathe /briːð/
cause /kɔːz/
cut down /kʌt'daʊn/
disappear /ˌdɪsə'pɪə^r/
increase /ɪnk'riːs/
melt /melt/
pick up /pɪk ʌp/
rise /raɪz/
waste /weɪst/

Nouns

increase /'ɪnkriːs/
island /'aɪlənd/
transport (n) /trænspɔːt/

Unit 5

American/British English

apartment /ə'pɑː^rtmənt/
flat /flæt/
elevator /'elɪveɪtə^r/
lift /lɪft/
garbage /'gɑː^rbɪdʒ/
rubbish /'rʌbɪʃ/
sidewalk /'saɪdwɔːk/
pavement /'peɪvmənt/
streetcar /'striːtkɑː^r/
tram /træm/
subway /'sʌbweɪ/
underground /'ʌndəgraʊnd/
vacation /və'keɪʃ^ən/
holiday /'hɒlədeɪ/

Verbs

make breakfast
/meɪk 'brekfəst/
switch off /swɪtʃ 'ɒf/

Nouns

baseball /'beɪsbɔːl/
career /kə'rɪə^r/
poem /'pəʊɪm/
poet /'pəʊɪt/
poetry /'pəʊɪtri/
population /ˌpɒpjə'leɪʃ^ən/
whale /weɪl/

Adverbs

already /ɔːl'redi/
just /dʒʌst/
yet /jet/

Everyday English

nice one! /'naɪs wʌn/
off we go! /ɒf wiː 'gəʊ/
sure /ʃɔː^r/
wicked! /'wɪkɪd/

Unit 6

Describing age

adult (n) /'ædʌlt/
age limit (n) /'eɪdʒ ˌlɪmɪt/
baby (n) /'beɪbi/
child (n) /tʃaɪld/
come of age (v) /kʌm əv
'eɪdʒ/
elderly (adj) /'eldəli/
middle-aged (adj)
/ˌmɪdl'eɪdʒd/
pensioner (n) /'penʃ^ənə^r/
teenager (n) /'tiːneɪdʒə^r/
toddler (n) /'tɒdlə^r/

Verbs

allow /ə'laʊ/
dress up /dres ʌp/
get married /ˌget 'mærɪd/
grow /grəʊ/
let /let/
prepare /prɪ'peə^r/
vote /vəʊt/

Nouns

bamboo /bæm'buː/
bungee jumping /'bʌndʒi
ˌdʒʌmpɪŋ/
ceremony /'serɪməni/
flag /flæg/
flame /fleɪm/
liana /li'ɑːnə/
music festival
/'mjuːzɪk ˌfestɪv^əl/
permission /pə'mɪʃ^ən/
rope /rəʊp/
torch /tɔːtʃ/
tourist /'tʊərɪst/
tower /'taʊə^r/

Adjectives

minimum /'mɪnɪməm/

Unit 7

Verb and noun pairs

have a drink /hæv ə 'drɪŋk/
have a (good) laugh
/hæv ə gʊd 'lɑːf/
have a good time
/hæv ə gʊd 'taɪm/
have fun /hæv 'fʌn/
make a fool of yourself
/meɪk ə 'fuːl əv jɔːˌself/
make a funny face
/meɪk ə ˌfʌni 'feɪs/
make a mistake
/meɪk ə mɪ'steɪk/
make fun of someone
/meɪk 'fʌn əv ˌsʌmwʌn/
make someone laugh
/meɪk ˌsʌmwʌn 'lɑːf/
make someone smile
/meɪk ˌsʌmwʌn 'smaɪl/

Verbs

examine /ɪg'zæmɪn/
frown /fraʊn/
laugh /lɑːf/
play the keyboard
/pleɪ ðə 'kiːbɔːd/
pretend /prɪ'tend/
smile /smaɪl/
worry /'wʌri/

Nouns

big deal /ˌbɪg 'diːl/
cash /kæʃ/
clown /klaʊn/
doctor /'dɒktə^r/
face /feɪs/
fancy dress /ˌfænsi 'dres/
fool /fuːl/
fun /fʌn/
hairstyle /'heəstaɪl/
hospital /'hɒspɪt^əl/
joke /dʒəʊk/
kid /kɪd/
landlord /'lænlɔːd/
laughter /'lɑːftə^r/
medicine /'meds^ən/
note /nəʊt/
nurse /nɜːs/
practical joke
/ˌpræktɪk^əl 'dʒəʊk/
rent /rent/
trouble /'trʌbl/

Adjectives

funny /'fʌni/
glad /glæd/

Everyday English

get a move on!
/get ə 'muːv ɒn/
I see /aɪ siː/

to be honest /tə biː 'ɒnɪst/
What do you reckon?
/wɒt də jə 'rek^ən/

Unit 8

Film

act (v) /ækt/
action film (n) /'ækʃ^ən fɪlm/
actor (n) /'æktə^r/
actress (n) /'æktrəs/
cameramen (n)
/'kæm^ərəmen/
cinema (n) /'sɪnəmə/
comedy (n) /'kɒmədi/
director (n) /dɪ'rektə^r/
drama (n) /'drɑːmə/
film set (n) /'fɪlm set/
film star (n) /'fɪlm stɑː^r/
horror film (n) /'hɒrə^r fɪlm/
image (n) /'ɪmɪdʒ/
movie (n) /'muːvi/
review (n, v) /rɪ'vjuː/
romance (n) /'rəʊmæns/
romantic (adj) /rə'mæntɪk/
scenery (n) /'siːn^əri/
science fiction (n)
/ˌsaɪəns 'fɪkʃ^ən/
screen (n) /skriːn/
script (n) /skrɪpt/
soundtrack (n) /'saʊntræk/
special effects (n)
/ˌspeʃ^əl ɪ'fekts/
star (v, n) /stɑː^r/
storyline (n) /'stɔːrɪlaɪn/
stunt (n) /stʌnt/
stuntwoman (n)
/'stʌntˌwʊmən/
theatre (n) /'θɪətə^r/
thriller (n) /θrɪlə^r/
western (n) /'westən/

Verbs

agree /ə'griː/
can't stand /kɑːnt 'stænd/
don't mind /dəʊnt 'maɪnd/
earn /ɜːn/
get up /ˌget 'ʌp/
hate /heɪt/
offer /'ɒfə^r/
prefer /prɪ'fɜː^r/
promise /'prɒmɪs/
refuse /ref'juːz/

Nouns

cosmetic surgery
/kɒzˌmetɪk 'sɜːdʒ^əri/
designer clothes
/dɪ'zaɪnə^r kləʊðz/
dream /driːm/
excitement /ɪk'saɪtmənt/
goldfish bowl /'gəʊldfɪʃ
bəʊl/
housework /'haʊswɜːk/
luxury /'lʌkʃəri/
magazine /ˌmægə'ziːn/

marriage /ˈmærɪdʒ/
nine-to-five job
    /ˌnaɪntəfaɪv ˈdʒɒb/
paparazzi /ˌpæpəˈrætsi/
photography /fəˈtɒgrəfi/
snake /sneɪk/

Adjectives

dangerous /ˈdeɪndʒərəs/
frightening /ˈfraɪtənɪŋ/
safe /seɪf/
terrifying /ˈterəfaɪŋ/

Unit 9

Disasters

ash (n) /æʃ/
avalanche (n) /ˈævəlɑːnʃ/
damage (v, n) /ˈdæmɪdʒ/
dead (adj) /ded/
destroy (v) /dɪˈstrɔɪ/
destruction (n) /dɪˈstrʌkʃən/
disaster (n) /dɪˈzɑːstər/
earthquake (n) /ˈɜːθkweɪk/
hit (v) /hɪt/
injure (v) /ˈɪndʒər/
knock down (v) /nɒk ˈdaʊn/
nuclear bomb (n)
    /ˌnjuːkliər ˈbɒm/
police rescue service (n)
    /pəˌliːs ˈreskjuː ˌsɜːvɪs/
rescue (v, n) /ˈreskjuː/
Richter scale (n)
    /ˈrɪktə skeɪl/
tsunami (n) /tsʊˈnɑːmi/
volcanic eruption
    /vɒlˈkænɪk ɪˈrʌpʃən/
volcano (n) /vɒlˈkeɪnəʊ/
winds (n) /wɪndz/

Verbs

blow off /bləʊ ˈɒf/
protect /prəˈtekt/
warn /wɔːn/

Nouns

building /ˈbɪldɪŋ/
cliff /klɪf/
coast /kəʊst/

Adjectives

alive /əˈlaɪv/
huge /hjuːdʒ/
lucky /ˈlʌki/
scared /skeəd/

Adverbs

luckily /ˈlʌkɪli/

Everyday English

get rid of (me) /get ˈrɪd əv/
(Joanne's) got a point
    /gɒt ə ˈpɔɪnt/
sort of /ˈsɔːt ɒv/
What's up with (her)? /wɒts
    ˈʌp wɪð/

Unit 10

Homes

block of flats (n) /blɒk əv
    ˈflæts/
bungalow (n) /ˈbʌŋgələʊ/
caravan (n) /ˈkærəvæn/
chimney (n) /ˈtʃɪmni/
cottage (n) /ˈkɒtɪdʒ/
detached (adj) /dɪˈtætʃt/
farm (n) /fɑːm/
floor (n) /flɔːr/
garage (n) /ˈgærɑːʒ/
garden (n) /ˈgɑːdən/
gate (n) /ˈgeɪt/
housing estate (n)
    /ˈhaʊzɪŋ ɪˌsteɪt/
lift (n) /lɪft/
longboat (n) /ˈlɒŋbəʊt/
longhouse (n) /ˈlɒŋhaʊs/
roof (n) /ruːf/
semi-detached (adj)
    /ˌsemidɪˈtætʃt/
stairs (n) /steəz/
swimming pool (n)
    /ˈswɪmɪŋ puːl/
tent (n) /tent/
terraced (adj) /ˈterɪst/
TV aerial (n) /ˌtiːˈviː ˈeəriəl/

Nouns

barbecue (n) /ˈbɑːbəkjuː/
down under /daʊn ˈʌndər/
jungle /ˈdʒʌŋgəl/
meal /miːl/
stereotype /ˈsteriətaɪp/
trek /trek/
tribe /traɪb/
visitor /ˈvɪzɪtər/
way of life /weɪ əv ˈlaɪf/

Adjectives

friendly /ˈfrendli/
good-humoured
    /ˌgʊdˈhjuːməd/
outdoor /ˌaʊtˈdɔːr/
relaxed /rɪˈlækst/
suntanned /ˈsʌntænd/

Unit 11

Remembering
and forgetting

forget (v) /fəˈget/
memorable (adj)
    /ˈmemərəbl/
memorise (v) /ˈmeməraɪz/
memory (n) /ˈmeməri/
remember (v) /rɪˈmembər/
remind (v) /rɪˈmaɪnd/

Determiners

all of them /ˈɔːl əv ðəm/
everyone /ˈevriwʌn/

everything /ˈevriθɪŋ/
everywhere /ˈevriweə/
none of them
    /ˈnʌn əv ðəm/
no one /ˈnəʊwʌn/
nothing /ˈnʌθɪŋ/
nowhere /ˈnəʊweə/
some of them
    /ˈsʌm əv ðəm/
someone /ˈsʌmwʌn/
something /ˈsʌmθɪŋ/
somewhere /ˈsʌmweə/

Verbs

improve /ɪmˈpruːv/
play from memory
    /ˌpleɪ frɒm ˈmeməri/
relax /rɪˈlæks/
revise /rɪˈvaɪz/

Nouns

advice /ədˈvaɪs/
architect /ˈɑːkɪtekt/
body /ˈbɒdi/
brain /breɪn/
grade /greɪd/
intelligence /ɪnˈtelɪdʒəns/
tip /tɪp/

Adjectives

interpersonal /ɪntəˈpɜːsənəl/
logical /ˈlɒdʒɪkəl/
mathematical
    /ˌmæθəˈmætɪkəl/
musical /ˈmjuːzɪkəl/
stressed /strest/
verbal /ˈvɜːbəl/
visual /ˈvɪʒuəl/

Everyday English

Come on! /kʌm ˈɒn/
I wonder ... /aɪ ˈwʌndə/
mates /meɪts/
Never mind! /ˈnevər maɪnd/

Unit 12

Music

album (n) /ˈælbəm/
boy band (n) /ˈbɔɪ bænd/
clarinet (n) /ˌklærɪˈnet/
classical (adj) /ˈklæsɪkəl/
concert (n) /ˈkɒnsət/
country (n) /ˈkʌntri/
disco (n) /ˈdɪskəʊ/
drums (n) /drʌmz/
electric guitar (n)
    /ɪˈlektrɪk gɪˈtɑːr/
electronic (adj)
    /ˌeləkˈtrɒnɪk/
fan (n) /fæn/
flute (n) /fluːt/
folk (n) /fəʊk/

headphones (n) /ˈhedfəʊnz/
heavy metal (n)
    /ˌhevi ˈmetəl/
hi-fi (n) /ˈhaɪfaɪ/
hit (n) /hɪt/
jazz (n) /dʒæz/
live (adj) /laɪv/
lyrics (n) /ˈlɪrɪks/
musical instrument (n)
    /ˌmjuːzɪkəl ˈɪnstrəmənt/
musician (n) /mjuːˈzɪʃən/
personal stereo (n)
    /ˌpɜːsənəl ˈsteriəʊ/
piano (n) /pjˈænəʊ/
practise (v) /ˈpræktɪs/
punk (n) /pʌŋk/
rap (n) /ræp/
rave (n) /reɪv/
recorded (adj) /rɪˈkɔːdɪd/
reggae (n) /ˈregeɪ/
rock 'n' roll (n) /ˌrɒkənˈrəʊl/
saxophone (n) /ˈsæksəfəʊn/
single (n) /ˈsɪŋgl/
stereo (n) /ˈsteriəʊ/
synthesiser (n) /ˈsɪnθəsaɪzər/
techno (n) /ˈteknəʊ/
trumpet (n) /ˈtrʌmpɪt/
violin (n) /vaɪəˈlɪn/
violinist (n) /vaɪəˈlɪnɪst/
voice (n) /vɔɪs/

Unit 13

Illness and medicine

ache (n) /eɪk/
ambulance (n) /ˈæmbjələns/
ankle (n) /ˈæŋkl/
antiseptic (n) /ˌæntɪˈseptɪk/
aspirin (n) /ˈæspərɪn/
chest (n) /tʃest/
cold (n) /kəʊld/
dentist (n) /ˈdentɪst/
doctor (n) /ˈdɒktər/
headache (n) /ˈhedeɪk/
health (n) /helθ/
heart (n) /hɑːt/
hospital (n) /ˈhɒspɪtəl/
hurt (v) /hɜːt/
medical (adj) /ˈmedɪkəl/
medicine (n) /ˈmedɪsɪn/
neck (n) /nek/
nurse (n) /nɜːs/
pain (n) /peɪn/
painful (adj) /ˈpeɪnfəl/
patient (n) /ˈpeɪʃənt/
penicillin (n) /ˌpenɪˈsɪlɪn/
sore (adj) /sɔːr/
stomach ache (n)
    /ˈstʌmək eɪk/
tablet (n) /ˈtæblət/
temperature (n)
    /ˈtemprətʃər/
throat (n) /θrəʊt/
toothache (n) /ˈtuːθeɪk/

transplant (n) /ˈtrænsplɑːnt/
treat (v) /triːt/
treatment (n) /ˈtriːtmənt/

Verbs

afford /əˈfɔːd/
suck /sʌk/

Nouns

chemical /ˈkemɪkəl/
herb /hɜːb/
hole /həʊl/
leech /liːtʃ/
member /ˈmembər/
Middle Ages /ˌmɪdl ˈeɪdʒɪz/
physics /ˈfɪzɪks/

Adjectives

ceramic /səˈræmɪk/
comic /ˈkɒmɪk/
common /ˈkɒmən/
cruel /ˈkruːəl/
horrible /ˈhɒrəbl/
radioactive /ˌreɪdɪəʊˈæktɪv/

Everyday English

Congratulations
    /kənˌgrætʃʊˈleɪʃənz/
end up with /end ˈʌp wɪð/
hang on to /hæŋ ˈɒn tə/
You're kidding! /jɔːr ˈkɪdɪŋ/

Unit 14

Computers

burn (v) /bɜːn/
CD drive (n) /ˌsiːˈdiː draɪv/
chat (v, n) /tʃæt/
chat room (n) /ˈtʃæt ruːm/
connect (v) /kəˈnekt/
connection (n) /kəˈnekʃən/
crash (v) /kræʃ/
disk drive (n) /ˈdɪsk draɪv/
download (v) /ˌdaʊnˈləʊd/
file (v, n) /faɪl/
hits (n) /hɪts/
IT (n) /ˌaɪˈtiː/
keyboard (n) /ˈkiːbɔːd/
laptop (n) /ˈlæptɒp/
link (v, n) /lɪŋk/
log on (v) /lɒg ˈɒn/
mouse (n) /maʊs/
mouse pad (n) /ˈmaʊs pæd/
net (n) /net/
offline (adv) /ɒfˈlaɪn/
online (adv) /ɒnˈlaɪn/
print (v) /prɪnt/
printer (n) /ˈprɪntər/
program (v, n) /ˈprəʊgræm/
provider (n) /prəˈvaɪdər/
publish (v) /ˈpʌblɪʃ/
save (v) /seɪv/
screen (n) /skriːn/
search (v) /sɜːtʃ/

search engine (n) /ˈsɜːtʃ
    ˌendʒɪn/
site (n) /saɪt/
software (n) /ˈsɒfweər/
surf (v) /sɜːf/
user (n) /juːzər/
website (n) /ˈwebsaɪt/

Verbs

change something for the
    better /tʃeɪndʒ ˌsʌmθɪŋ fə
    ðə ˈbetər/
provide /prəˈvaɪd/
rely on /rɪˈlaɪ ɒn/
start up /stɑːt ˈʌp/
work something out /wɜːk
    ˌsʌmθɪŋ ˈaʊt/

Nouns

addiction /əˈdɪkʃən/
employee /ɪmˈplɔɪiː/
eyesight /ˈaɪsaɪt/
importance /ɪmˈpɔːtəns/
injuries /ˈɪndʒəriz/
inspiration /ˌɪnspərˈeɪʃən/
project /ˈprɒdʒekt/
success /səkˈses/

Adjectives

addicted /əˈdɪktɪd/
independent
    /ˌɪndɪˈpendənt/
psychological
    /ˌsaɪkəlˈɒdʒɪkəl/
stressful /ˈstresfʊl/

Unit 15

Noun suffixes -r, -er, -ist, and -or

archaeologist
    /ˌɑːkiˈɒlədʒɪst/
artist /ˈɑːtɪst/
cyclist /ˈsaɪklɪst/
decorator /ˈdekəreɪtər/
driver /ˈdraɪvər/
explorer /ɪksˈplɔːrər/
farmer /ˈfɑːmər/
footballer /ˈfʊtbɔːlər/
journalist /ˈdʒɜːnəlɪst/
owner /ˈəʊnər/
photographer /fəˈtɒgrəfər/
professor /prəˈfesər/
receptionist /rɪˈsepʃənɪst/
scientist /ˈsaɪəntɪst/

Nouns

archaeology /ˌɑːkiˈɒlədʒi/
civilisation /ˌsɪvəlaɪˈzeɪʃən/
discovery /dɪˈskʌvəri/
empire /ˈempaɪər/
expedition /ˌekspɪˈdɪʃən/
explanation /ˌekspləˈneɪʃən/
figure /ˈfɪgər/

journal /ˈdʒɜːnəl/
kitten /ˈkɪtən/
ladder /ˈlædər/
ruins /ˈruːɪnz/
sand /sænd/
square /skweər/
temple /ˈtempl/
window cleaner
    /ˈwɪndəʊ ˌkliːnər/

Adjectives

royal /ˈrɔɪəl/
terracotta /ˌterəˈkɒtə/
tropical /ˈtrɒpɪkəl/

Everyday English

give it a go /gɪv ɪt ə ˈgəʊ/
good luck /gʊd ˈlʌk/
stuff /stʌf/
though /ðəʊ/

Unit 16

Noun suffixes -ation and -ment

calculation /ˌkælkjəˈleɪʃən/
communication
    /kəˌmjuːnɪˈkeɪʃən/
education /ˌedjʊˈkeɪʃən/
entertainment
    /ˌentəˈteɪnmənt/
equipment /ɪˈkwɪpmənt/
improvement
    /ɪmˈpruːvmənt/
information /ˌɪnfəˈmeɪʃən/
management
    /ˈmænɪdʒmənt/

Verbs

apologise /əˈpɒlədʒaɪz/
arrange /əˈreɪndʒ/
calculate /ˈkælkjəleɪt/
communicate
    /kəˈmjuːnɪkeɪt/
educate /ˈedʊkeɪt/
entertain /entəˈteɪn/
equip /ɪˈkwɪp/
improve /ɪmˈpruːv/
inform /ɪnˈfɔːm/
manage /ˈmænɪdʒ/
spill /spɪl/
touch /tʌtʃ/

Nouns

airport /ˈeəpɔːt/
bad luck /ˌbæd ˈlʌk/
conversation
    /ˌkɒnvəˈseɪʃən/
devil /ˈdevəl/
horseshoe /ˈhɔːsʃuː/
lucky break /ˌlʌki ˈbreɪk/
manager /ˈmænɪdʒər/
mirror /ˈmɪrər/
moon /muːn/

performance /pəˈfɔːməns/
shoeshine boy /ˈʃuːʃaɪn bɔɪ/
shoulder /ˈʃəʊldər/
spirit /ˈspɪrɪt/
superstition /ˌsuːpəˈstɪʃən/
witch /wɪtʃ/

Adjectives

evil /ˈiːvəl/
superstitious /ˌsuːpəˈstɪʃəs/